ANGLESEY CHURCHES

Anglesey Churches

Geraint I.L. Jones

ISBN: 1-84527-089-4
Cover design: Sian Parri

First published in 2006 by
Gwasg Carreg Gwalch, 12 Iard yr Orsaf,
Llanrwst, Wales LL26 0EH
01492 642031 01492 641502
books@carreg-gwalch.co.uk Internet: www.carreg-gwalch.co.uk

ACKNOWLEDGEMENTS

My sincere thanks to the Reverend J. Gareth Parry for sharing some of his encyclopaedic knowledge of matters relating to the Anglican Church and specific Anglesey churches. Also to my sister Gwenllian for her patience and support, and to the Ynys Môn Records Office, Llangefni for assistance.

GLOSSARY OF WELSH PLACE-NAMES

Amlwch Port	Porth Amlwch
Beaumaris	Biwmares
Bull Bay	Porth Llechog
Holyhead	Caergybi
Menai Bridge	Porthaethwy
Newborough	Niwbwrch
Puffin Island	Ynys Seiriol
Valley	Y Fali

CONTENTS

Chapter 1
INTRODUCTION

The island of Anglesey was continuously occupied by the Romans from 78 AD to 410 AD. The conquest of the island, which they named Mona, was met with stiff resistance from the native Druidic people. The Romans defeated them and this marks the end of the power of the Druid priests. Christianity reached Wales during the centuries of Roman rule; at first the Romans sought to ban the new faith but it gradually came to be accepted. However, when the Romans left in 410, Wales was still largely pagan. Traces of the Roman presence in Anglesey are not numerous; a notable example is the third century Roman Fort at Holyhead. One must remember that at this time, the political division of southern Britain into Wales and England was yet to occur. The inhabitants are referred to as Britons and they spoke a language which was a precursor of the Welsh language.

Following the Roman period, from about 449 AD, the conquests of the Teutonic Anglo-Saxons in what is now the south and east of England drove the Britons to the west. A number of English kingdoms emerged and in 829 King Egbert came to be regarded as the first overall King of England. The Britons, at first under the control of various princes struggling for supremacy in their own areas, were later to form the nation of Wales. Offa's Dyke was built between 757 and 796 and this was part of the process whereby the land to the west emerged as a nation. Thus we see a clear distinction developing between two parts of Britain that we now recognise as Wales and England.

In the centuries following the departure of the Romans, Wales was christianised by the Celtic Saints. A saint could be described as a man or woman who lived a simple life that is devoted to God. Comparatively little is known about most of them; it is also difficult to separate fact from legend. Sometimes these saints established monasteries (e.g. Penmon and Holyhead). Other saints were simply wandering monks who established hermit cells very often in remote places in the mountains or on islands (e.g. Ynys Seiriol/Puffin Island). These cells would often be on round (or oval) plots of land; this explains why some Anglesey churchyards are roughly circular. These cells might later become a cluster of buildings (a *Llan*). The primitive churches would eventually become more elaborate wooden buildings and sometimes larger settlements would develop around them. A number of large churches (e.g. St Cybi, Holyhead) were Welsh monasteries or *clasau* (see Chapter 3). In Wales there are hundreds of place-names containing the word *Llan* and this is evidence for the great industry of the early Christian saints and the profound influence they must have had. Christianity was well-established in Wales and other western parts of Britain by about 600, but the Teutonic tribes in the south-east of Britain were yet to be converted.

Later in the 9th and 10th centuries, all parts of Britain, including Anglesey, were subject to raids by the pagan Vikings from Scandinavia. The Vikings attacked and burnt St Seiriol's church at Penmon in 971 AD. Evidence of the Viking presence in Anglesey is sparse, although the name 'Anglesey' itself is of Scandinavian origin. The Vikings had their own Norse gods, but they embraced Christianity in the 11th century.

In 1066, William the Conqueror defeated the Anglo-Saxon King Harold at the Battle of Hastings, and the Normans then ruled England. The Normans later made inroads into Wales, and their castles are testimony to their supremacy. The Normans were noted for their architecture and there are churches in Anglesey today which show the influence of Norman styles. It was at about this time that it became normal practice to build stone churches. Such churches would be very rudimentary and would normally have a thatched roof, an earth floor but no seating. Worshippers would have to stand during services. The Normans did not approve of the Welsh clas churches with their married priests and sought to enforce a celibate priesthood and continental-style monasteries. This opened the door for the Benedictine and later the Cistercian monasteries.

The Christian church was ultimately controlled from Rome with the Pope as its head. Latin was its universal language. Rome's supremacy was challenged from time to time, but in Britain it was Henry VIII (reigned 1509-1547) who broke away from the control of Rome. He did this because the Pope would not allow him to divorce his first wife, Catherine of Aragon, so that he could marry Anne Boleyn. Henry VIII declared himself Supreme Head of the Church of England. This change heralded the beginning of the Protestant Reformation. The Bible was translated into English and copies placed in the churches in 1539; this Bible has been subsequently revised a number of times. Henry VIII also initiated the Dissolution of the Monasteries from 1538 onwards and in Anglesey the monastery at Llanfaes was affected. Some monasteries were in a state of decline by this time and their closure did not create widespread opposition. As the Protestant Reformation gained momentum, Catholics increasingly faced persecution and a number of Welsh Catholics were put to death for practising their faith.

The Act of Union of 1536 joined Wales to England. In 1567 William Salisbury translated the New Testament into Welsh. At the request of Queen Elizabeth I, Dr William Morgan later translated the complete Bible into Welsh; this was seen as a means of drawing the Welsh people into the Protestant faith. His work was published in 1588 and it is undoubtedly a significant factor in the survival of the Welsh language in the centuries that followed.

The Civil War (1642-1648) saw the overthrow and execution of King Charles I. This was followed by a republican period known as the Commonwealth (1648-1660) under Oliver Cromwell before the monarchy was restored. During Cromwell's rule a number of religious Dissenters (later to be known as Nonconformists) emerged; they challenged the doctrines of the Church of England. After the restoration of the monarchy in 1660, measures were taken against these Dissenters. In Wales the Baptists and the Quakers were persecuted and many were forced to leave for America. By 1689, however, the Act of Tolerance allowed religious freedom to the Dissenters. This period saw the building of the first chapels in Wales.

As time went on, Anglican churches became more elaborate. By the 17th century wooden seating was provided – simple benches for the poor, but the gentry might expect their own box-pews. Floors of tiles or slabs came a little later. By the 19th century all church roofs were of slate or lead.

In 18th century Wales, a Methodist Revival was led by Howel Harris (1714-1773), Daniel Rowland (1713-1790) and others. The Methodist Revival was initially a movement within the Church of England. It was Thomas Charles (1755-1814), usually associated with Bala, who took the Welsh Methodists out of the Anglican Church in 1811 so that they then joined the ranks of other Nonconformists. This was a period dominated by the great preachers, of whom Christmas Evans (1766-1838) was arguably the most famous. During the nineteenth century the growth of Nonconformity in Wales was phenomenal and vast numbers of chapels were built across the length and breadth of the country. Such was the scale of the growth of Nonconformity that in Anglesey alone about 73 chapels (of various denominations) were built between 1800 and 1840.

The Anglican Church in Wales, on the other hand, seemed to be in decline at the beginning of the 19th century. Only two new churches (Amlwch and Llangefni) were built between 1800 and 1840. The Church also suffered from the effects of absentee priests and priests who spoke no Welsh. In addition, many churches were situated in remote places, far from the most populous villages. Developments such as the building of the A5 road by Thomas Telford (completed in the 1820s) and the subsequent development of the railway caused population shifts that led to the building of a number of new churches during the period 1840 to 1900, for example at Llanidan (1841), Bryngwran (1841), Gaerwen (1847), Llanfair Pwllgwyngyll (1853), Menai Bridge (1858), Cemaes (1865) and Valley (1867). During this period a handful of new 'mission churches' and 'mission rooms' were also built; their purpose was to bring the church closer to the people in areas where there was previously no church. Examples can be found at Newborough, Malltraeth and Bull Bay (Porth Llechog).

During the Victorian period church restoration became very

fashionable throughout Britain, and Anglesey was no exception. Henry Edward Kennedy, the Bangor diocesan architect, was responsible for much of the designing and building work, sometimes in collaboration with others. The similarity of style which many of the island's churches share is partly due to Kennedy's work. Kennedy was active from the early 1840s until about 1894, when he was succeeded as diocesan architect by Peter Shearson Gregory. In a few parishes, surprisingly, rebuilding work was in the hands of the clergy themselves and several 19th century incumbents took an active part in this work. A very significant part was also played by the wealthy landowning families of the period – the Stanley family (of Holyhead), the Bulkeleys (of Baron Hill, Beaumaris) and a number of others were generous benefactors to a number of churches during the 19th century. Without their generosity much of the restoration work would not have been possible. Unfortunately, not all the restoration work carried out in the 19th century is now regarded as satisfactory – some noteworthy features (e.g. rood screens) in a number of churches were lost during this period.

By the end of the 19th century, the Anglican Church had addressed most of its shortcomings. Most of the clergy were bilingual and some new churches had been built closer to the centres of population, but by 1900 such was the growth of the Nonconformist Denominations that Anglicans were in a minority.

Sixteenth century laws had prevented Catholics from openly exercising their faith, but such laws had been removed by the Catholic Emancipation Act of 1829. The Catholic hierarchy (bishops and archbishops) was restored in Britain in 1850. Anglesey's first Catholic church (at Holyhead) was built in 1860. All of the island's Catholic churches are now housed in purpose-built 20th century buildings.

In 1920, under the Disestablishment Act, the Welsh Anglican Church was separated from the Church of England, and the Church in Wales was created. Anglesey's Anglican Churches are part of the Diocese of Bangor, established under St Deiniol about 546. Traditionally, the island is divided into rural deaneries and subsequently into parishes. These divisions have undergone changes from time to time, but this is outside the scope of this small volume which is concerned with the Churches themselves. The Roman Catholic Churches of Anglesey are part of the Catholic Diocese of Wrexham (established in 1987 to include all the north Wales counties and the Montgomery district of Powys).

The 20th century saw a further decline in the fortunes of the Anglican church in terms of dwindling congregations and the closure of churches. In 1930 there were 93 Anglican churches in use in Anglesey but in 2006 the number of open churches has declined to 75. This latter figure includes 8 churches where services are only conducted occasionally. Most of those which have closed were the smaller rural churches or those in areas (e.g. Holyhead) where there was more than one church. But it is true to say that Nonconformist congregations have also declined and a considerable number of chapels have closed – very different from the days of the famous religious revival (*Y Diwygiad*) of 1904-05 led by Evan Roberts and his charismatic followers. As we enter the twenty-first century and the third millennium, the Christian denominations are all facing their toughest challenge – the increasingly secular nature of Welsh society.

The reader will notice that the alphabetical section (Chapter 4) contains a considerably longer entry for some churches than others. The reason is simple – some churches are more historic than others. A few Anglesey churches have significant historical associations, possibly stretching over many centuries, whereas others have comparatively little. Some churches are built on sites established by the Celtic saints in the 6th or 7th centuries; others are far more recent and have no such history. Many of the older churches are a product of different periods. The information given in the alphabetical section is based upon the architectural style of the windows, the doors, the roof beams and the general construction of the church. Other features, such as fonts and pulpits, can be roughly dated according to their style.

We should remember that churches are part of the community they serve, and that they reflect the history of that community. The church of St Credifael, Penmynydd, for example, is closely linked to the Tudors of Plas Penmynydd. Many other churches are also linked to powerful local dynasties, many of which have ceased to exist. Sometimes churches contain some surprising items; for example, there are a few Anglesey churches (Llanedwen, Llaneilian and Penmynydd) that contain dog-tongs. They would be used in the days when it was acceptable and, indeed, not unusual to take dogs to church. This practice was widespread in Wales. If dogs started to fight, they would be unceremoniously grabbed by the use of tongs and thrown out!

At the beginning of the twenty-first century the various Christian churches and chapels find it increasingly difficult to maintain their ministry and their buildings. The only truly historic buildings are the older Anglican churches. The oldest nonconformist chapels date only from the eighteenth century and most are nineteenth century buildings. The Catholic churches (with the exception of Beaumaris and Amlwch) are from the latter part of the twentieth century. The current condition of many of the island's Anglican churches gives some cause for concern. It is certainly true that the Church in Wales has restored a number of churches and continues to do so. However, the sheer number of churches involved, the small congregations and the shortage of funds makes this an increasingly difficult task. This is all the more difficult when one considers that according to the Census of 2001, fewer than one in ten of the population of Wales attend a place of worship. Many of our most historic churches, some of which are Grade 1 or 2 listed buildings, will need a great deal of expensive restoration if they are to be preserved for the future.

Chapter 2
NAMES OF CHURCHES

A number of Anglesey Churches bear the names of Celtic Saints (e.g. Llanbadrig, Llandysilio etc), although some churches are dedicated to saints from the scriptures (e.g. Peter and Mary). It is quite possible that these latter churches were originally established by Celtic saints, but that their names were later changed to names which were perceived to be more fashionable, possibly through the influence of the Normans who were particularly faithful to Rome.

As we have seen the Welsh word *Llan* originally meant 'a clearing' or 'a plot of consecrated land', but later came to mean 'a church' or 'the settlement immediately surrounding a church'. Many Welsh place names are made up of *Llan* followed by the name of the saint to whom the church is dedicated, e.g.

Llan + Saint Sadwrn	becomes	Llansadwrn
Llan + Saint Pabo	becomes	Llanbabo
Llan + Saint Trygarn	becomes	Llandrygarn

The change which occurs in the initial consonant of the saint's name in some instances is called a mutation, a characteristic feature of the Welsh language. Not every Llan is named after a saint. For example, Llangefni takes its name from a geographical feature, the river Cefni, and not from Saint Cyngar to whom the church is dedicated. Similarly Saint Cawrdaf's Church is in the parish of Llangoed. The names of some parishes do not contain the *Llan* element at all, e.g. Saint Credifael's church is in the parish of Penmynydd.

Where churches are dedicated to more than one saint, the parishes can be called Llanddeusant (two saints) or Llantrisant (three saints), but the saints' names are not individually specified in these cases. Several Anglesey churches are dedicated to female saints, e.g. Saint Dona (Llanddona), Saint Ceinwen (Llangeinwen). This reflects the fact that women must have had a significant part to play in the early Christian church.

Churches dedicated to scriptural saints, such as Mary (Mair) and Michael (Mihangel) tend to be very numerous. In order to distinguish between them, an additional territorial description is usually added, e.g. Llanfihangel Tre'r Beirdd (*Church of St Michael in the Township of the Poets*); Llanfihangel yn Nhowyn (*Church of St Michael in the Duneland*), Llanfihangel Din Sylwy (*Church of St Michael near the Fort of the Sylwy tribe*).

There are often inconsistencies in the spelling of a number of saints' names and parish names. These are ancient names and have been variously spelt over the centuries. Examples include Llanfigel/Llanfigael, Llanfihangel Esgeifiog/Llanfihangel Ysgeifiog. Purists may often favour one spelling in preference to others and efforts have been made to standardise spellings, but considerable variations are still encountered.

Chapter 3
SOME TECHNICAL TERMS

No two churches are exactly alike, but there are many features which churches have in common. Readers who are unfamiliar with church architecture would be advised to study this chapter as well as Figures 1-4 which show simple plans and drawings for commonly-encountered types of church. This book is not intended to be a manual on church architecture or practice but it is appropriate to explain terms which will frequently be used in Chapter 4. Not all these features, of course, will be relevant for a particular church.

Aisle Passage between rows of pews.

Altar Communion table, located in chancel in the eastern end of a church.

Altar rail Wooden or metal rail which separates the altar from the remainder of the chancel.

Ambry Closed recess in wall of church for storing communion vessels etc.

Apse Semi-circular end of a part of a church.

Arcade Series of arches to support the roof.

Belfry Space inside church tower where bells are located. The sound escapes through louvred panels.

Bell-cote A housing for the church bell(s) as found in small churches, usually in the west end of a church.

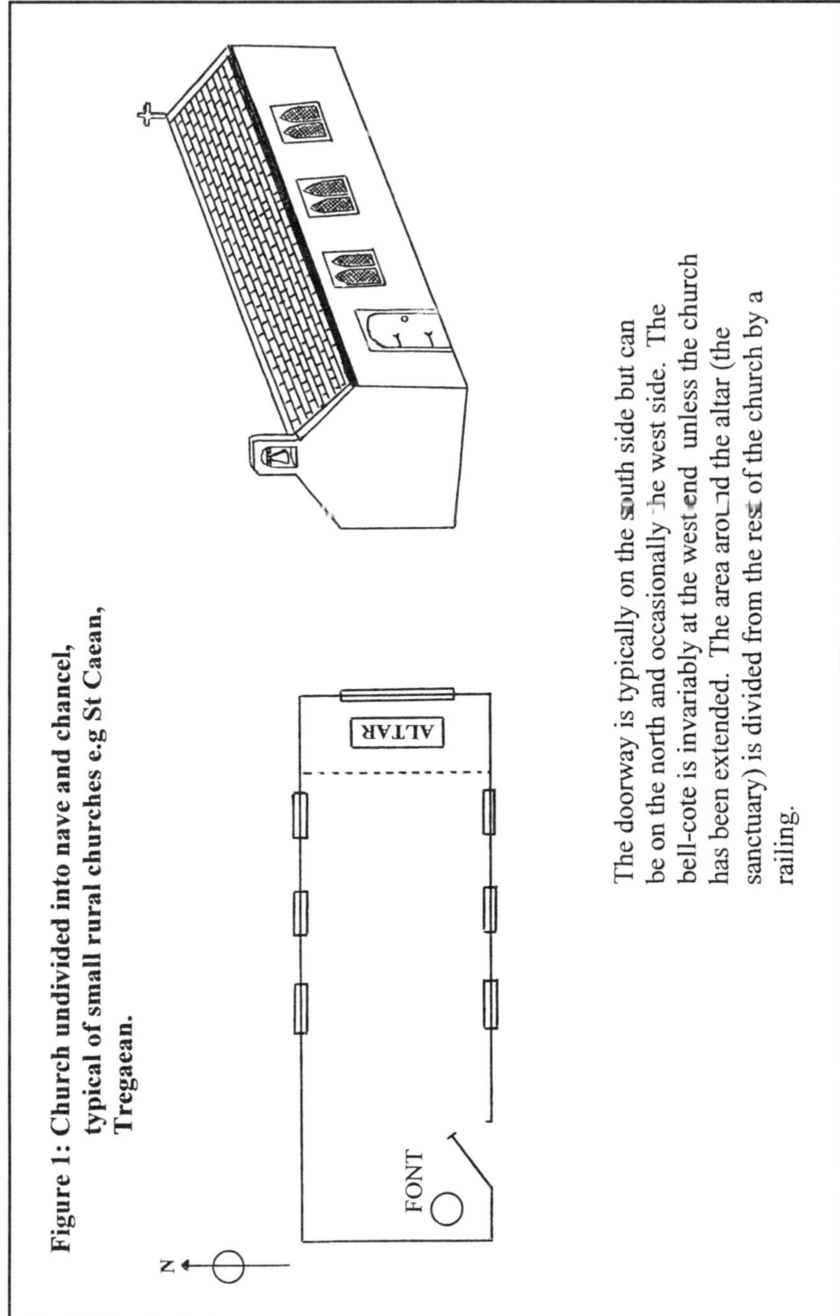

Figure 1: Church undivided into nave and chancel, typical of small rural churches e.g St Caean, Tregaean.

The doorway is typically on the south side but can be on the north and occasionally the west side. The bell-cote is invariably at the west end unless the church has been extended. The area around the altar (the sanctuary) is divided from the rest of the church by a railing.

Bulwark Low wall at the edge of the roof; sometimes plain but sometimes decorated e.g. castellated (like the walls of a castle).

Buttress Support built against a wall to increase its strength.

Chapel In architectural terms, a chapel is an extension of the chancel on the north or south side of a church.

Chapel of Ease Subordinate church, located for convenience of local parishioners.

Chancel Eastern part of a church, reserved for clergy, choir etc and often separated by a screen. The organ is usually in the chancel.

Chancel arch Arch inside a church which separates nave and chancel.

Chests Used to store alms, parish registers, wills or other records.

Chevron stone Stone bearing chevron markings (i.e. zig-zags), much used in 12th century architecture as decoration.

Choir stalls Area in chancel reserved for church choir.

Clas A traditional Celtic monastery church which functioned as a mother church with a number of associated subsidiary churches, e.g. St Cybi, Holyhead, and Llaneilian. The clas system was not favoured by the Normans who sought to disband it and replace it with continental style monasteries.

Corbel Stone projecting from wall to support roof timbers. In some churches they are ornately carved.

Figure 2: Church having a separate nave and chancel and a porch on the south side, e.g. St Beuno, Trefdraeth.

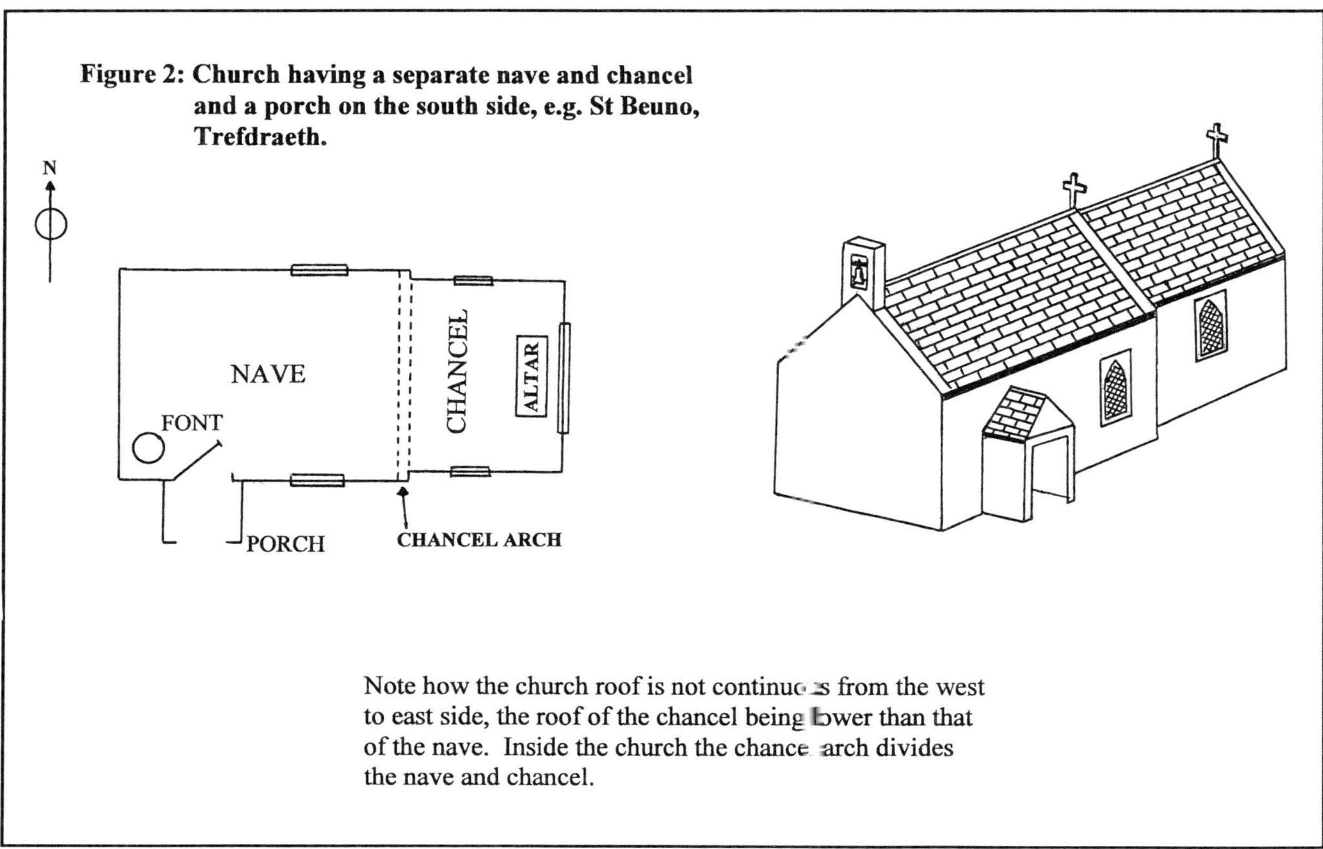

Note how the church roof is not continuous from the west to east side, the roof of the chancel being lower than that of the nave. Inside the church the chancel arch divides the nave and chancel.

Cruciform church Church built in the form of a cross.

Crypt Underground vault which could be used for burials.

Door The main door is typically situated in the south of a church, but doors can also be found in the west and in the north.

Drip stone Projecting stone to keep rain from parts below.

Font Receptacle for baptismal water, usually found near the door of the church (i.e. the west end).

Gargoyle Grotesque water spout through which water from church roof and guttering is discharged. Carvings have open mouths through which the water drains.

Gothic Architectural style from 12th to 16th century with pointed arches.

Gritstone A coarse sandstone, much used for making fonts.

Lancet window Narrow window (or part of window) with pointed head. Where 2 or 3 lancets make up a complete window, it is known as a double or triple lancet.

Lectern Desk where Bible is placed.

Light Vertical section of a divided window, e.g. a window might be described as being in 3 lights.

Lychgate Roofed gateway of churchyard where traditionally at a funeral the coffin awaits arrival of priest. Any form of arched gateway is regarded as a lychgate.

Figure 3: A cruciform church (i.e. church in the shape of a cross), e.g. St Cawrdaf, Llangoed.

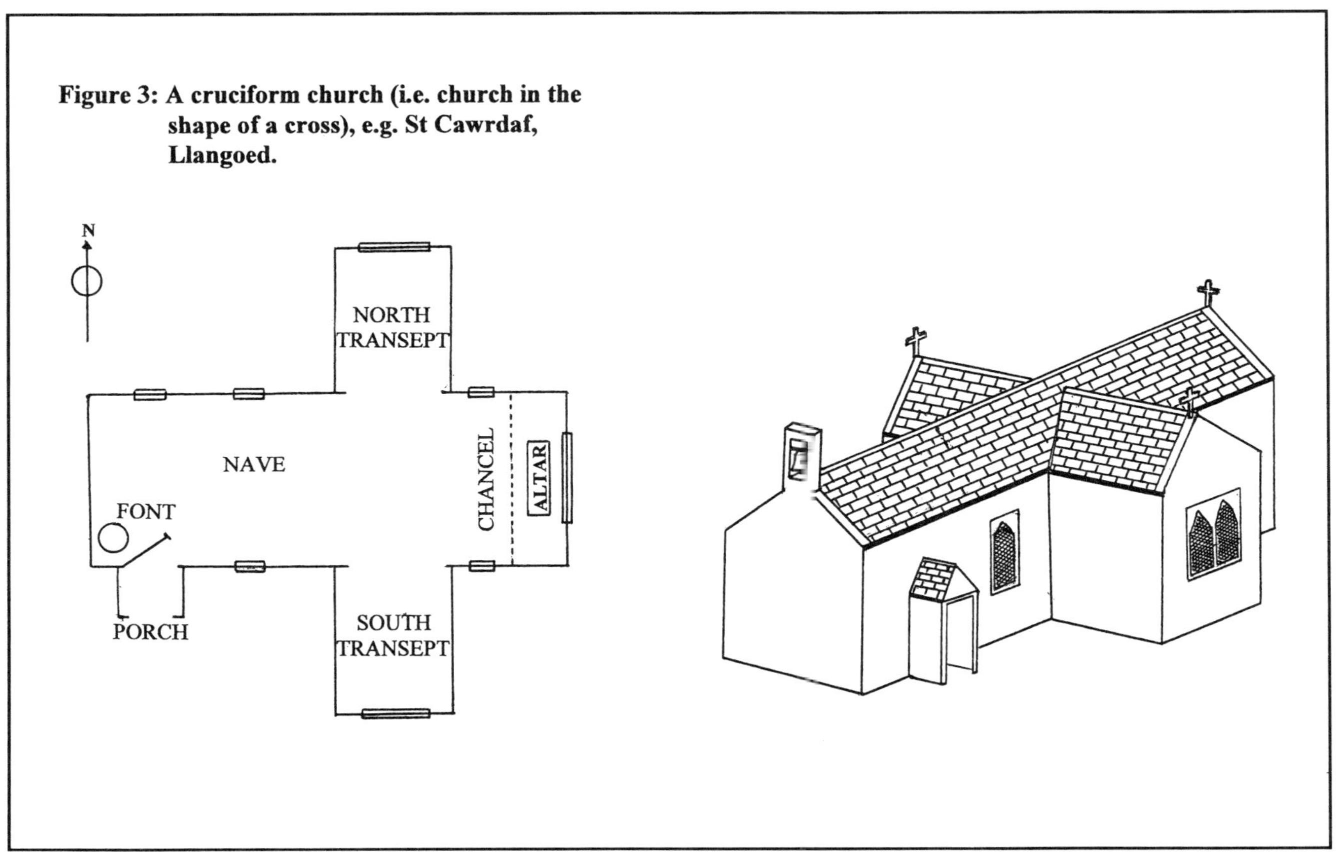

Minstrel's Gallery	Area in church reserved for musicians, normally in the west of a church. This practice goes back to times when small churches did not have an organ.
Misericords	Hinged seats to give support to a person standing during long services.
Mounting block	Stone block to facilitate the mounting of a horse, often seen outside rural churches.
Nave	Body of church from west door to chancel, usually separated by pillars from aisles.
Norwich Taxation	The Norwich Taxation is a survey of parish churches and their land. The documents relate to 1253-54.
Piscina	Stone basin used to carry away water used in rinsing chalice and other vessels.
Porch	Covered approach to door normally, though not always, situated in the south side of a church.
Pulpit	Raised area from which the priest delivers the sermon.
Quatrefoil	Shape in window resembling four-lobed leaf or flower.
Reredos	Decorated screen or wall decoration situated behind the altar.
Rood screen	Carved screen of wood or stone separating nave and chancel.
Sanctuary	Region of chancel in the immediate vicinity of the altar.

Figure 4: A church having a north chapel and a north porch e.g. St Morhaiarn, Trewalchmai

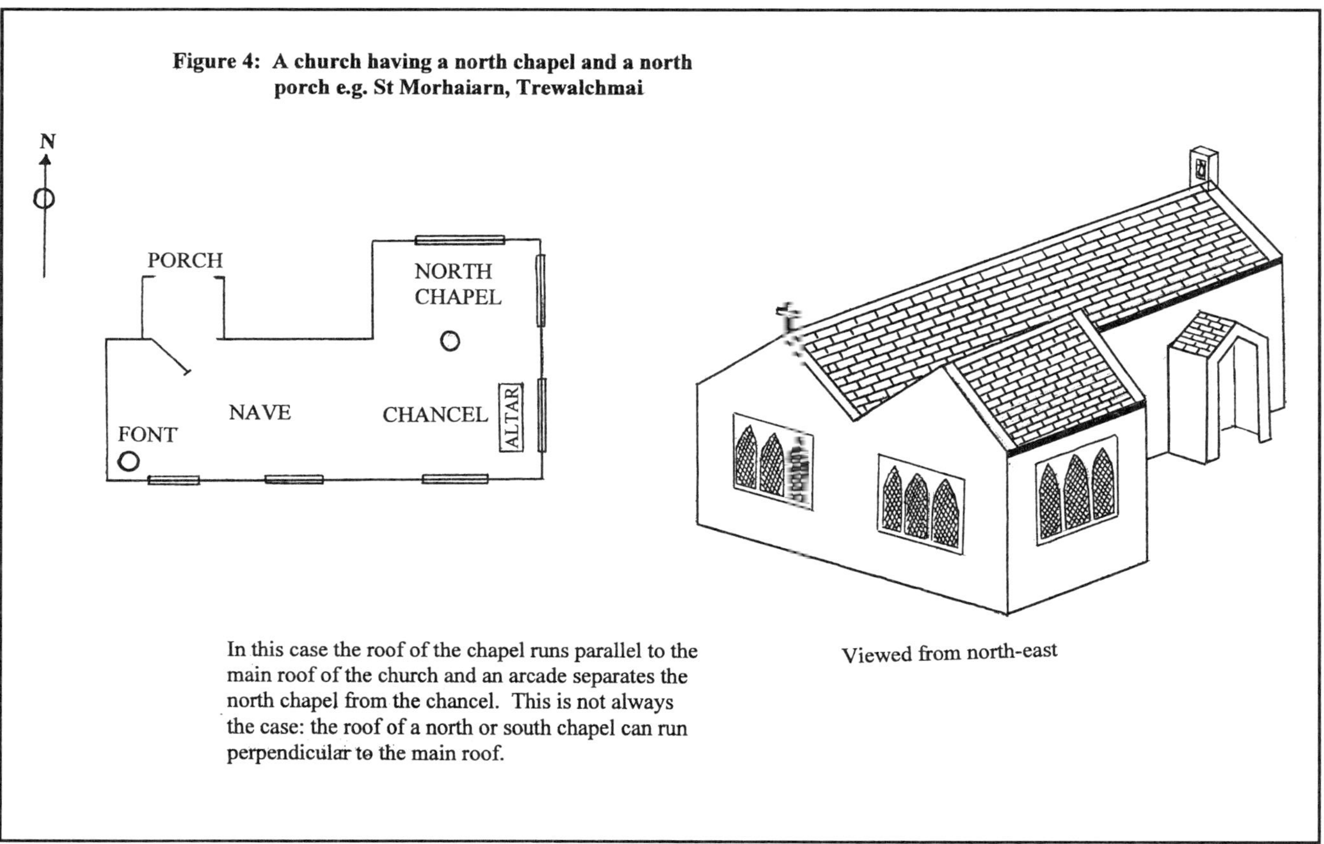

In this case the roof of the chapel runs parallel to the main roof of the church and an arcade separates the north chapel from the chancel. This is not always the case: the roof of a north or south chapel can run perpendicular to the main roof.

Spire Conical or pyramidal structure above church tower.

Stained glass Ornate windows used to enhance appearance of a church. Normally they depict Biblical scenes.

Stoup Hollowed stone to hold holy water. In pre-Reformation times it was the practice for worshippers to use this water to make a sign of the cross before entering the church. After the Reformation this practice was discontinued, but ancient stoups are still to be seen in some churches.

Tower Found on the west side or the middle of a church and sometimes containing a clock.

Tracery Ornamental stonework e.g. in head of window.

Transept Transverse parts of a cruciform church. Individually known as the north and south transepts.

Vestry Room attached to a church where vestments are stored and put on.

Weather -vane Often sited at the highest point of a church.

Chapter 4
ALPHABETICAL SECTION

This section does not attempt to detail every church building that has ever existed in Anglesey; its main purpose is to list those churches which are now in use and those which have been used in recent times or are of historical interest. Those churches which have closed or no longer exist are described as such.

It should be borne in mind that very few churches are now left unlocked. Sometimes access to view a church can be obtained by contacting a keyholder. Notice boards outside individual churches sometimes give this information.

In relation to some churches, mention is made of a society known as The Friends of Friendless Churches. This charity, formed in 1957 and based in London, takes responsibility for the restoration and upkeep of some churches which are no longer in regular use. The society has been especially active in Wales.

Nowadays it is common practice for several parishes to be grouped together as a benefice; this has meant that individual parishes do not have the same importance and significance as in times gone by. In this volume Anglican churches are listed under the traditional parishes and cross-indexed under location; the Catholic churches are listed according to location only. If the buildings or the sites still exist, they are numbered and the map in Figure 5 shows their location. Every care has been taken to check the facts presented in this section but the reader should bear in mind that churches (and what is contained in them) can change over a period of time.

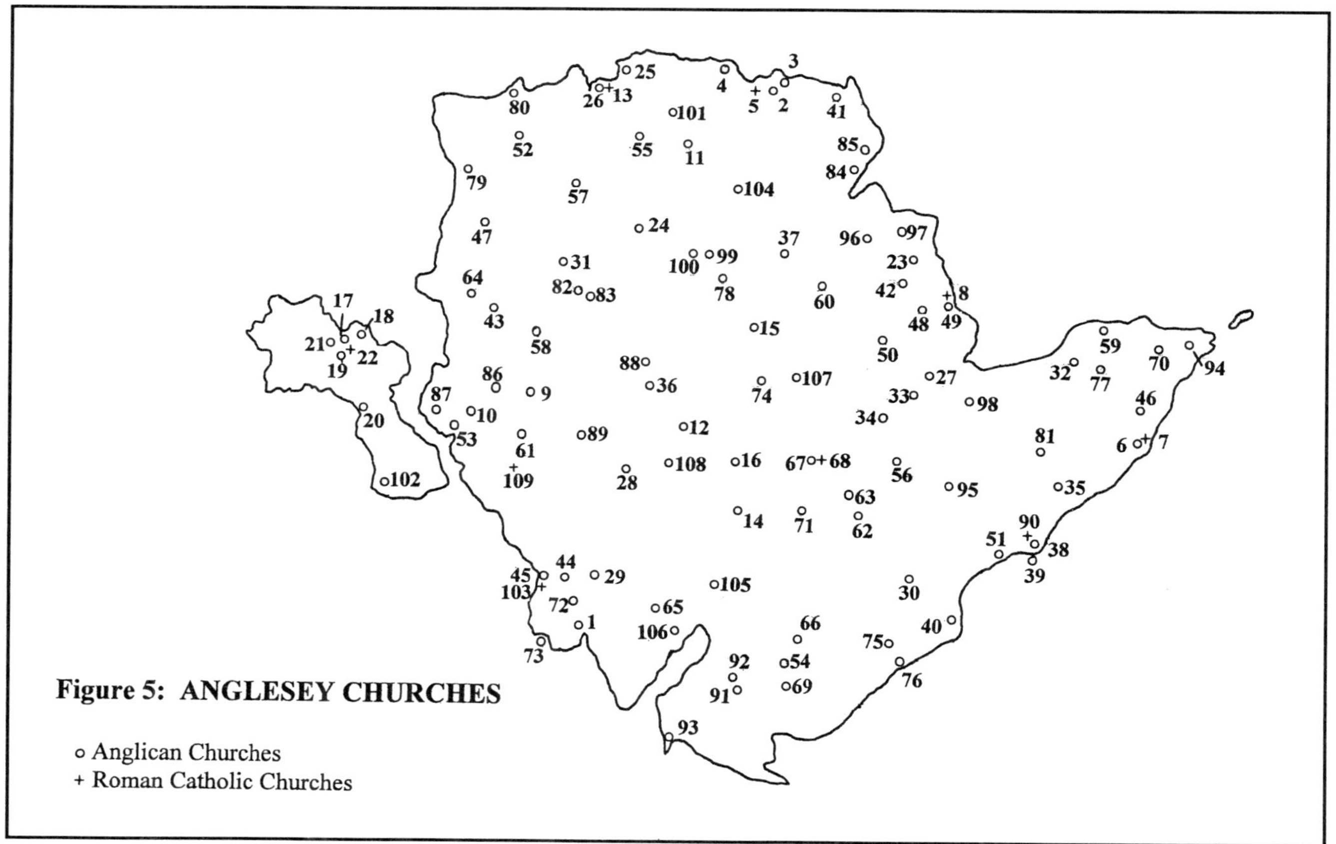

Figure 5: ANGLESEY CHURCHES

Aberffraw – *St Beuno*

St Beuno's Church stands next to the primary school in the middle of the village. Grid Reference SH 353 688.

The religious cell was established here early in the 7th century by Saint Beuno who later became the Abbot of Clynnog Fawr on the Llŷn peninsula. In the 12th century a stone church was built, but was only about half the width of the present church. Aberffraw assumed importance as the site of the chief court of the Princes of Gwynedd. The present church which contains traces of 12th century masonry in the south wall of the nave may have been a royal chapel. It is unusual as it is double-aisled, with the north aisle and the four-arch arcade dating from the 16th century. The church was restored in 1840 when general repairs and re-roofing took place. The exterior walls were partly rebuilt in 1868. The south porch (around the 14th century doorway) and the north vestry were both added in 1868 also. Some repair work was undertaken in 1950. In the west wall a 12th century semicircular Romanesque arch decorated with chevrons and animal heads has been set and this is believed to be the chancel arch of the original church. It was discovered by the rector, the Reverend Hugh Wynne Jones, during the 1840 restoration. The octagonal font is medieval. The bell-cote contains two bells set one above the other; both bear the date 1896. The north, south and east walls contain stained glass. All the windows are modern but some on the south side are badly weathered. A new plain gate leads into the large churchyard where, on the south side, many of the gravestones (probably the oldest ones in the churchyard) have been laid flat. Aberffraw church has a long history and is an interesting one to view. [1]

Amlwch – *St Eleth*

St Eleth's church is situated in Amlwch town centre.
Grid Reference SH 442 929.

This large church is dedicated to St Eleth, a 6th century saint who had a holy well at Amlwch Port. Two previous churches are said to have been struck by lightning. The church became too small for the rapidly increasing population of Amlwch in the boom years of copper extraction at Mynydd Parys. In 1787 Thomas Williams (Twm Chwarae Teg, also known as the Copper King) offered £600 towards the cost of building a new church. The new church, in a Georgian style, was not built until 1800. The cost of its construction was about £2,500 with significant contributions from the companies that mined Parys Mountain. Considerable rebuilding was undertaken in the 1860s. A large lychgate leads into the churchyard where all the gravestones have been lifted and moved to the sides, presumably for ease of maintenance. It is a spacious, high sided building with an impressive tower. The shape of the building is unusual and not typical of Anglesey churches generally. The tower contains a belfry (with two bells dated 1687 and 1820), and a one-faced clock; it is topped by four weather vanes and a flagpole. The doorway is at the base of the tower. The east window contains stained glass, but the other windows contain clear leaded glass. The font is modern, dating from 1900. Under the supervision of architect Adam Voelcker, the church underwent extensive refurbishment in 1999 including a new balcony. It is a good example of a tastefully restored church. [2]

Amlwch – *Port Church. St Peter/Sant Pedr*

This church is situated in Llewelyn Street, Amlwch Port.
Grid Reference SH 453 932.

St Peter's Church is often referred to simply as the Port Church. It was built for the seafaring families of Amlwch Port. It is a small building completed in 1871 at a cost of £662. It has a bell-cote and a porch on the west side of the building. The church was taken out of service in June, 1981, because of dry rot. After extensive restoration it was reopened in May 1987 with replacement furniture from the redundant St Elbod's Church in Holyhead. The church became redundant in the 1990s and is now privately owned. [3]

Amlwch – *Bull Bay Mission Room/ Ystafell Genhadol Porth Llechog*

The former mission room is at the bottom of a steep hill, a short distance from the A5025. Grid Reference SH 426 943.

The Bull Bay Mission Room (which is within the Parish of Amlwch) dates from the 1890s and was in use until the 1970s. It is now in private ownership and has been converted into dwellings; it is barely recognisable as a former church building. [4]

Amlwch – *Catholic Church of our Lady Star of the Sea and St Winefride/Eglwys Gatholig Mair Seren y Môr a Santes Wenfrewi*

Amlwch's Catholic Church stands in a prominent position on the A5025, about half a mile west of the town centre. Grid Reference SH 438 931.

Amlwch's Roman Catholic Church is a very impressive building and must surely be the most unusual church in Anglesey. The foundations for the church were excavated in 1932 and it was completed and consecrated in 1937. It was designed by an Italian architect. The church is a reinforced concrete building in the shape of an upturned boat; underneath the church is a large parish hall for social activities. Behind the altar, the reredos is a massive hollowed half cone about 6m tall. In the roof is a series of windows which provide continuous light from one side of the church to the other. At one end of the church high above the door is a star-shaped window, and there are five smaller such windows in the wall of the chancel. At the time of writing the church is closed for renovations, the worshippers attending services at Cemaes and Benllech. [5]

Beaumaris – *St Mary & St Nicholas/ Santes Fair & Sant Nicolas*

This church is situated in Church Street. Grid Reference SH 604 762.

The town of Beaumaris was created by King Edward I after his conquest of Wales. The original church dates from the early 14th century and was originally a garrison church for the castle. At this time it was a chapel of ease to Llandegfan church. It was dedicated to St Mary and to St Nicholas, the patron saint of sailors. This would seem to be appropriate as Beaumaris was one of the busiest ports in Europe in medieval times. It is the only church in the diocese of Bangor dedicated to St Nicholas. The nave and the north and south aisles date from this period. It was rebuilt and enlarged in 1500 and embellished with castellated parapets; the chancel was also rebuilt at this time. In the 1810s the upper part of the tower was rebuilt to house six bells (later increased to eight) donated by the seventh Viscount Bulkeley. The town clock (with four faces) was also installed at this time. In 1825 it was further restored at a cost of £312 and new windows were fitted in the tower. Further restoration occurred in 1902. The roof underwent repairs in 1927. The church is now a grade 1 listed building (Figure 6). The south porch and the north vestry are fairly modern. The south porch of the church contains an empty stone coffin with a carved lid; it is said to be the coffin of Siwan (or Joan), daughter of King John of England and the wife of Llewelyn ap Iorwerth, who died in 1237. The carving on the lid shows an effigy of Princess Siwan. The location of Siwan's remains is not known. The coffin was originally at the Franciscan monastery at Llanfaes, but has been at Beaumaris church since 1929. Slate tablets in the porch testify (in Welsh, English and Latin) that the coffin was saved from the indignity of being used as a horse trough by Viscount Bulkeley in 1808. He placed it in a mausoleum at Baron Hill, from where it eventually came to the church. Also in the porch stands a black wooden watchman's box which was used during the body-snatching scare of the early 19th century. Inside the church are two arcades to separate the aisles, as well as a pipe organ. There are numerous old gravestones to be seen in the floor. The church also contains a fine example of an alabaster table tomb which can be found at the west end of the north aisle. According to some, this is a memorial to local magnate Sir Rowland Bulkeley (died 1537) and his wife Alice Beaconsall. Others claim that it is the tomb of William Bulkeley (died about 1490) and his wife Elen Gruffydd. The tomb probably came from the monastery at Llanfaes and may have been removed at the time of the dissolution of the monasteries in 1538. The choir stalls in the chancel with their carved misericords, dating from around 1500, are of considerable interest. They are among the finest examples anywhere in Britain.

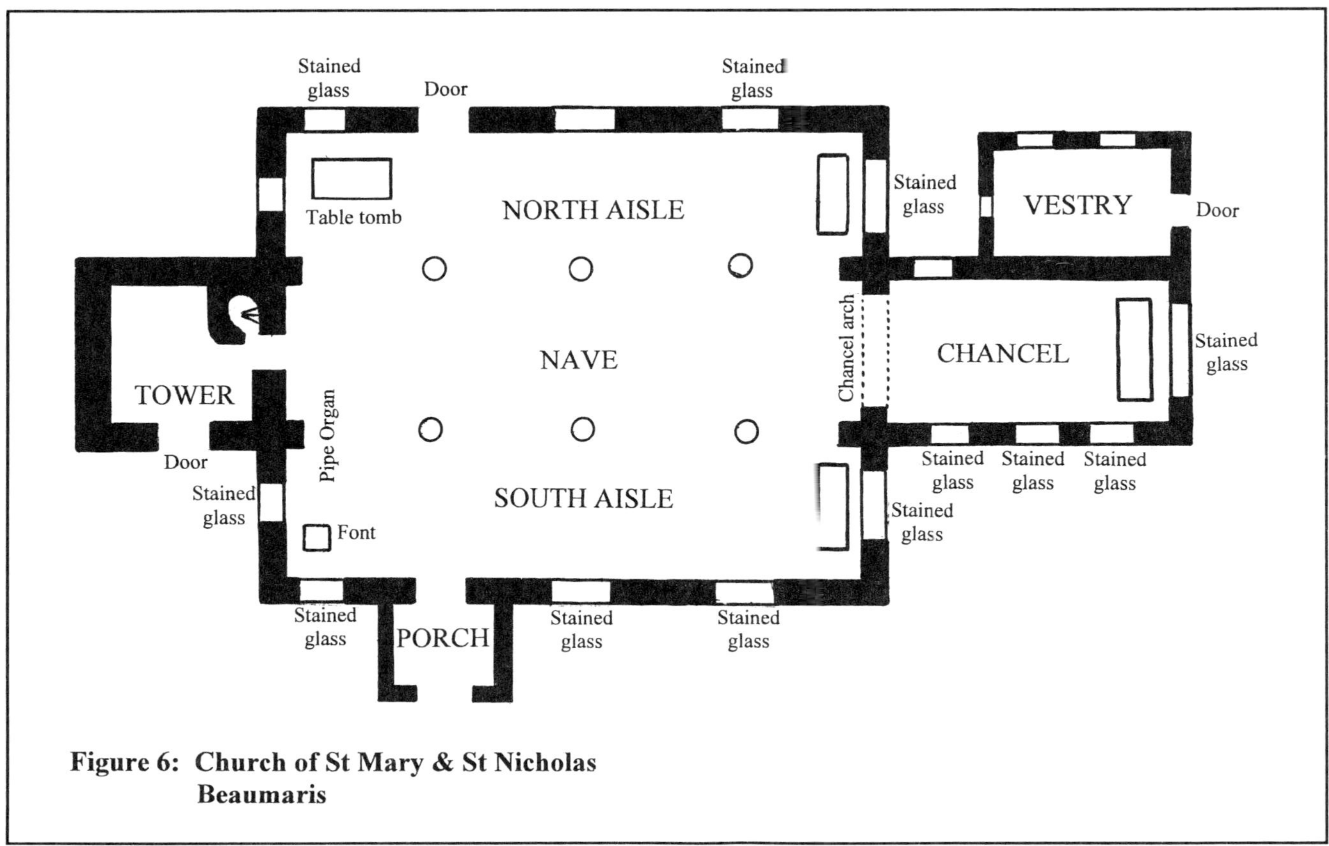

Figure 6: Church of St Mary & St Nicholas Beaumaris

It is believed that the misericords may have come from Llanfaes, but it is also possible that they may have been made specially for this church. The twenty misericords depict various scenes of medieval life; there are 12 different carvings. They underwent restoration in 2004. There are a considerable number of stained glass windows, the east window of the chancel (in memory of Richard Williams Bulkeley who died in 1918) being particularly impressive. All the stained glass is modern except the fragments in the south window of the sanctuary; these are probably 15th century. On the north wall of the chancel is a memorial tablet to David Hughes, who came from a poor family in Llantrisant but became a successful businessman. He contributed financially to the establishment, in 1603, of the Grammar School in Beaumaris. He died in 1609 and was buried in Norfolk. In the east and south parts of the churchyard are a number of old gravestones. Famous botanist and priest Hugh Davies (1739-1821), author of 'Welsh Botanology', is buried in the churchyard. Inside the church, on the south wall of the chancel, is a tablet to his memory. [6]

Beaumaris – *Our Lady Queen of the Seas Roman Catholic Church/Eglwys Babyddol ein Harglwyddes Brenhines y Moroedd*

Beaumaris Catholic Church is situated in Rating Row, a short distance from the castle. Grid Reference SH 606 762.

There was a Catholic presence in Beaumaris at the very end of the 19th century, but the present church was not built until 1909. This small neat-looking church stands on a small grassy plot with no burials. It is not aligned in the usual east-west direction like most churches. It is built of dark stone with sandstone windows. Most of the windows have clear leaded glass. There is a round window in the chancel and the window above the porch has some particularly ornate tracery. It is the oldest of the island's Catholic churches and the only one built in a traditional church style. [7]

Benllech – *St Andrew/Sant Andreas*

(see Llanfair Mathafarn Eithaf)

Benllech – *Our Lady of Lourdes Roman Catholic Church/Eglwys Gatholig ein Harglwyddes o Lourdes*

This church is on Beach road, a short distance from the village square. Grid Reference SH 520 828.

This church was completed in 1965 and is a modern whitewashed building of unusual shape which is mostly under a flat roof. Part of the building has a steeply-pitched slate roof. It is surrounded by lawns. [8]

Bodedern – *St Edern*

The church stands next to the B5109 in the centre of the village. Grid Reference SH 333 804.

The name Bodedern means the 'dwelling of Edern'. St Edern established his church in the 6th century. The site of the original church may have been at Pen Eglwys Edern, about half a mile south east of the present church. The lychgate leads directly from the street to the churchyard. The present church is the result of the extensive restoration in 1871 by Henry Kennedy of the older 14th century church at a cost of about £1000. This is when the chancel was added and the old east window reset in the new extension. Original features such as the 15th century south doorway and several 15th century windows were also preserved. There is also a 14th century north door in the nave. The bell-cote contains one bell, probably 17th century. The roof timbers are medieval. The octagonal font is also believed to be medieval. At the west end is a minstrel's gallery supported by oak cross beams and bearing the date 1777. There are ornate wood carvings between the nave and chancel; these came from Jesus College, Oxford with which Bodedern had a connection from the 17th century onwards. Inside the church can also be found an ancient inscribed stone bearing the name of a person called Ercagni (or Erchan). It is believed to date from the period 475-525 AD and was discovered nearby at Arfryn, Bodedern in 1972. Long-cist graves (where bodies were buried in coffins made of flat stones) were also found at Arfryn. The stained-glass window in the north chapel commemorates the Reverend John Wynne Jones, who was the first Vicar of Bodedern from 1868 to 1888. Previous incumbents had always been curates.

One of the figures in the window (Simeon) bears a deliberate resemblance to the Reverend Jones. There is also stained glass in the south and east windows of the chancel. All other windows contain clear leaded glass. [9]

Bodedern – *St David/Dewi Sant, Caergeiliog*

The church stands next to the A5 in the centre of the village of Caergeiliog. Grid Reference SH 311 784.

This church, in an 'Arts and Crafts' style, was built about 1910 (and just within the traditional parish of Bodedern) to serve the community of Caergeiliog on the A5 road and is situated in an elevated position near the roadside. It did not replace any other church building and the site has no previous religious significance. The building stands on a small plot and there is one gravestone on the north side. St David's church serves both as a church and a church hall. The bell-cote and the porch are on the west side. Above the porch there is a white cross and to the right of the porch a stone bearing a Celtic cross has been set in the wall. All the windows are of clear leaded glass but there is some stained glass in the east window. This window bears the inscription: 'In memory of those who gave their lives in defence of freedom'. Inside the church there are both pews and chairs. A large hinged screen can be used to open and close the area around the altar. [10]

Bodewryd – *St Mary/Santes Fair*

This church is situated on a minor road between Llanfechell and Rhosgoch. Grid Reference SH 400 906.

The name Boderwyd means 'the dwelling of Erwyd (or Gerwyd)'. St Mary's church stands near the roadside in a pleasant location. It is one of the smallest churches in Anglesey and was once a chapel of ease to Llaneilian church. A small gate leads to a footpath terminating at an archway over a heavy wooden gate. The church stands in a circular churchyard. The bell-cote contains one bell dated 1747. The nave and chancel are continuous and the east wall contains a 16th century window. The other windows are modern. The porch is on the north side and is a modern addition. The present church replaced a previous church struck by lightning.

The building work was made possible by money donated by Henry Edward John Stanley, the third Baron Stanley of Alderley (1827-1903). Since he was a Muslim, the church contains some features of Islamic design such as the design of the stained-glass windows. [11]

Bodffordd – *St Llwydian* (see Heneglwys)

Bodwrog – *St Twrog*
The church is situated on a minor road between Llynfaes and Gwalchmai. Grid Reference SH 400 776.
The tiny church of St Twrog stands near the roadside in an elevated spot in a remote rural location. A small gate leads to the churchyard. The present church was built in the 15th century and has undergone partial restoration. It is undivided into nave and chancel. The east window, which is plainly of some antiquity and much weathered, dates from the 16th century. There was once a north doorway, but it has been converted into a window. The north and south walls contain windows from the 15th century (at the eastern end) as well as more modern windows from the 17th/18th century. There is no stained glass and all the windows contain clear glass. There is a stone bearing the image of a bull's head over the 16th century south door. The bell-cote contains one bell dated 1668. The building appears to be in fairly good condition. The roof is slated with unusually large old slates. Inside, the pews, pulpit and other fittings are painted a cream colour. There is an oak collecting shovel dated 1733. The interior is lit by gas lamps. [12]

Bryngwran – *Holy Trinity Church/Eglwys y Drindod Sanctaidd* (see Llechylched with Ceirchog)

Brynsiencyn – *St Nidan (New Church)* (see Llanidan)

Brynsiencyn – *St Nidan (Old Church)* (see Llanidan)

Bull Bay (Porth Llechog) – *Mission Room/Ystafell Genhadol* (see Amlwch)

Caergeiliog – *St David/Dewi Sant* (see Bodedern)

Ceirchiog – *Betws y Grog (Holy Rood Church)*
Grid Reference SH 361 769.
This church was closed in about 1843 when the parish was amalgamated with Llechylched. Holy Trinity Church in Bryngwran then became the parish church. The walled enclosure of the Holy Rood church, overgrown with trees, can still be seen not far from the A55 and A5. Within this enclosure some tombs are still evident although the church itself is no longer visible.

Cemaes – *St Padrig* (New Church) (see Llanbadrig)

Cemaes – *St David's Roman Catholic Church/ Eglwys Babyddol Dewi Sant*
The church is situated in Athol Street, not far from the harbour.
Grid Reference SH 371 935.
St David's Church was opened in March 1965 on a site near the centre of the village. It was built with volunteer labour and has room for 140 worshippers. It is a fairly small white brick building with a tiled roof. A small white statue of St David is near the doorway. Previously, Roman Catholics had worshipped in a room at a local public house known as The Old Vigour (situated nearby) since 1942. [13]

Cerrigceinwen – *St Ceinwen*
The church is situated 0.5 mile from the village of Llangristiolus.
Grid Reference SH 424 737.
St Ceinwen was the daughter of Brychan Brycheiniog and the sister of St Dwynwen (see Llanddwyn) and St Dyfnan (see Llanddyfnan). The cell was first established here in the 7th century. The church is set in a hollow and access is through a small gate and a sloping path. There is a spring in the south side of the churchyard; this is St Ceinwen's well which was once believed to have healing properties. Parts of the north side of the churchyard are very overgrown. The bell-cote is particularly large and houses one bell. All the windows are of coloured leaded glass; there is no

stained glass. The circular tub-shaped font dates from the 12th century (on a modern base); it features carved panels. There is a gravestone set in the ground near the door; it is believed to be 1100 years old. Another incised gravestone set in the wall above the door is 800 years old. On one wall can be seen the gravestone of Morris Lloyd, a Royalist who was killed by Cromwell's soldiers in 1647. The church underwent some building work in 1839 but the present church dates from 1860, the architects being Henry Kennedy and Frederick Rogers. [14]

Coedana – *St Ana (Anau)*

This church is situated about 2 miles (3km) south of Llannerch-y-medd on the B5111. Grid Reference SH 431 822.

This small church, once a chapel of ease to Llaneilian church, stands at the roadside in a rural location. When the B5111 road was improved in the 1960s, the new road passed on the east side of the church, leaving the old road on the west side. The church is of neat appearance and the churchyard, which contains a number of small yew trees, is well-maintained. The church, which is divided into nave and chancel, was rebuilt in 1892. The windows of the north and south side contain frosted leaded glass. The east window is in three lights and contains coloured glass. The bell-cote contains one bell. The porch is on the south side. The stonework of the church is of a slightly different appearance on the north side, being redder in colour. The cylindrical font dates from 1702. [15]

Gaerwen – *St Michael/Sant Mihangel*

(see Llanfihangel Esgeifiog)

Gaerwen – *Church of Jesus Christ of the Latter-day Saints*

This church stands next to the A5 road in the village of Gaerwen, not far from the Post Office. Grid Reference SH 482 719.

The Church of Jesus Christ of Latter-day Saints (the Mormon Church) was established in the USA in 1830. Records show that as early as the 1840s and 1850s there were a small number of Mormons in Anglesey. In the 1970s Mormons worshipped for a time at Llangristiolus Community Hall and later at Llangefni. The present Mormon chapel was completed in 1985 and replaced a temporary building which had been on the same site since 1981. It is a brown brick building with a tiled roof. It incorporates a family history centre.

Gwalchmai – *St Morhaiarn* (see Trewalchmai)

Gwredog – *St Mary/Santes Fair* (see Rhodogeidio)

Heneglwys – *St Llwydian*

The church is situated about 1 mile (1.5 km) south of the village of Bodffordd on the road which connects the B5109 and the A5. Grid Reference SH 423 761.

In the past Heneglwys has also been called Llan y Saint Llwydion (Church of the Grey Saints) and Mynwent Corbre (Corbre's cemetery). An arched gateway leads to the neat churchyard. The present church was rebuilt in 1845 on the foundations of the previous church and using some material from the previous building. The Rector, the Reverend J. Wynne Jones, was the architect. Further restorátion took place in 1896, the architect being Peter S. Gregory. The church is undivided into nave and chancel. The south porch contains a 14th century doorway. The bell-cote contains two bells but has space for three. The windows in the north and south walls are very old, probably from the 14th or 15th century. They are windows in three lights containing leaded glass, some coloured and some clear. The more modern east window is also in three lights and contains stained glass. The style of the carved stones set in the walls (above the south porch, north door and high above the east window) suggests that they date from the 12th century. The font is a 12th century circular bowl. [16]

Holyhead – *St Cybi*

The church is situated in a prominent position not far from the A5 and the harbour. Grid Reference SH 247 826.

About 550 AD St Cybi, who is believed to have been the son of a Cornish chieftain, built a monastery within the walls of a 3rd or 4th century Roman fort. It is believed that the land was given to him by Maelgwn Gwynedd. The early church was plundered by Vikings in 967, although the monastery itself survived into the 13th century. St Cybi's church was a monastic clas church with associated parishes at Bodedern, Bodwrog and Llandrygarn. The present church building (Figure 7) has its origins in the 12th or 13th century although most of it dates from the 15th and 16th centuries. The chancel is from the 13th century. The church was enlarged, the north and south transepts being added about 1480 and the north aisle about 1500. The south aisle and the south porch were added about 1520. Some of the castellated parapets were also added at about this time. They are decorated with various emblems and human faces. The tower dates from the 17th century and the vestry in the north-west corner dates from 1817. The tower is topped by a squat slated pyramid. The weather vane (with a fish design) on the tower bears the date 1753. The two bells date from 1625 and 1801. There is a sundial on the south wall of the south transept. The church was completely restored in 1877-79 to designs by renowned architect Sir George Gilbert Scott (1811-1878). The church roofs were reconstructed in 1814 and 1877-79; they are mostly covered with lead. The chancel roof, however, is of slate with red ridge tiles. The late Victorian Stanley Chapel (a Welsh inscription below its east window notes its completion in 1897) contains stained-glass windows by William Morris and Sir Edward Burne-Jones. One of these windows depicts the 'Tree of Life'. The Stanley Chapel is named after William Owen Stanley (1802-1884), a Lord Lieutenant of Anglesey, MP for Anglesey, scholar and one of Holyhead's most generous benefactors. He gave £3000 for the restoration of St Cybi's church. The chapel contains a memorial to William Owen Stanley and his wife Ellen. The tomb is of Italian Carrara marble and depicts a recumbent figure guarded by angels. On the west wall is a plaque from the Netherlands which commemorates the Dutch servicemen who were in Holyhead during the Second World War. Near the vestry is an oak singer's seat which would once have been occupied by singers trained to lead the congregation during hymn-singing. An unusual feature is the lepers' window which allowed lepers to see inside the church and follow the services without entering the

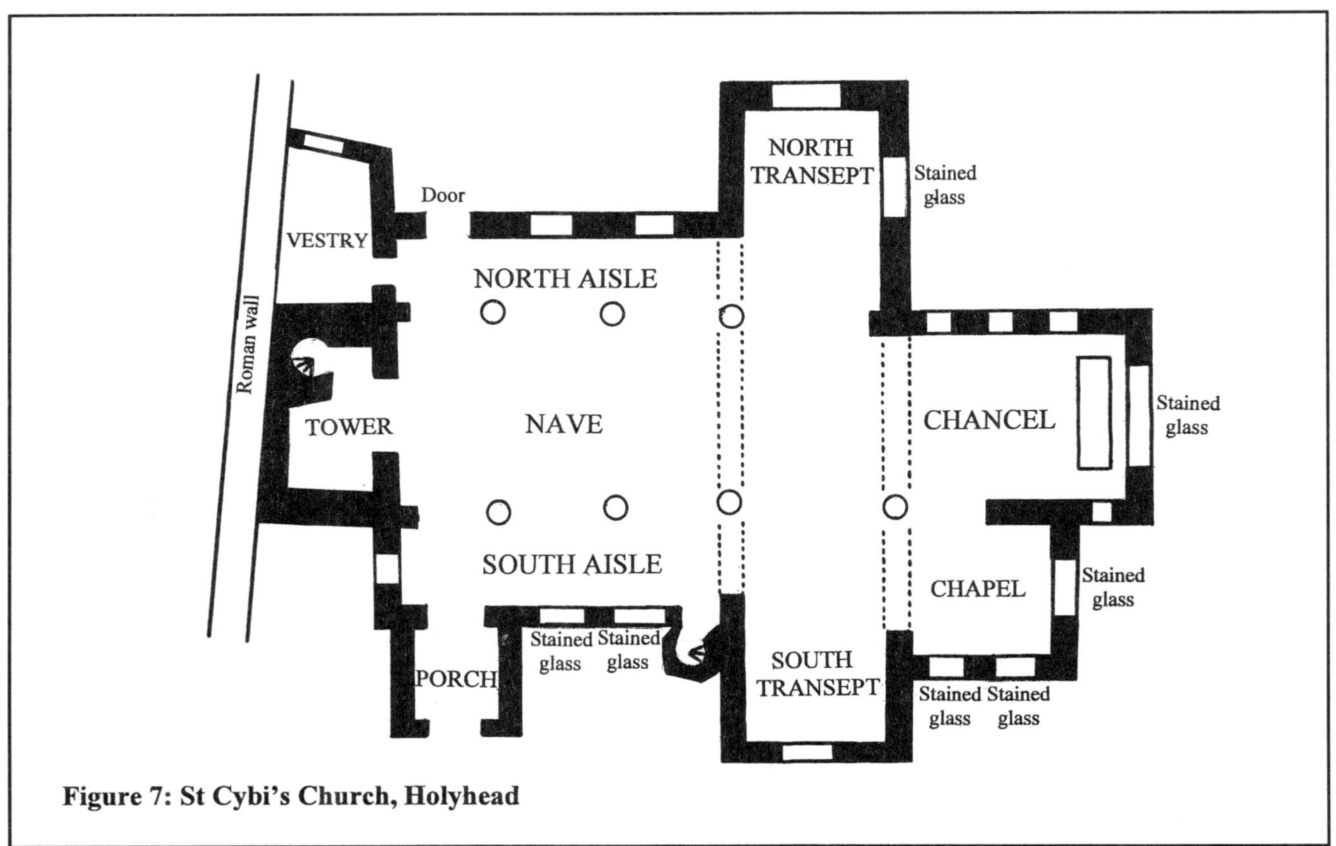

Figure 7: St Cybi's Church, Holyhead

church and mixing with the congregation. The font is an octagonal bowl dated 1662. St Cybi's church has a number of other features which make it one of the most interesting in Anglesey. [17]

Holyhead – *St David/Dewi Sant (Morawelon)*
Grid Reference SH 253 822.
This is a modern building which was erected in the 1960s. It serves the large Morawelon housing estate. The building functions as a church, church room and meeting hall. It was dedicated to St David in the early 1990s, having previously been known simply as Morawelon. [18]

Holyhead – *Eglwys y Bedd*
This tiny church is situated next to St Cybi's Church.
Grid Reference SH 247 826
The 14th century chapel of Eglwys y Bedd (Church of the Grave), which stands near St Cybi's church, may have been the original site of St Cybi's cell. It is also known as Llan y Gwyddel. The original building was longer. Only the nave of the original church now remains; the chancel arch can be seen in the exterior wall surrounding the door. The building once housed the first school in Holyhead (1748 onwards) which was founded by Thomas Ellis (1711-1792), the rector of St Cybi's church in the mid-18th century. It was restored in 1980 and is now used as a church room. Eglwys y Bedd reputedly contains the grave of Seregri, a 5th century leader of Irish warriors repelled from Anglesey by Cadwallon Lawhir, a Welsh Chieftain.

Holyhead – *St Elbod*
St Elbod's Church was situated in Rhos y Gaer Avenue.
Grid Reference SH 246 820.
St Elbod's was a small church intended to serve a particular part of the town. It was designed by well-known architect Harold Hughes and completed in 1905. It was closed in the 1980s, and was later converted into a museum. It now houses a number of apartments (known as St Elbod's Court), but its ecclesiastical style is still apparent. [19]

Holyhead – *St Ffraid/Santes Ffraid, Trearddur Bay*
This church is situated in the village at the side of the B4545.
Grid Reference SH 259 788.
The original church was built on a nearby site but had to be abandoned because of erosion by the sea in the 1870s. A wooden church was subsequently erected in 1893 at Porth y Post. This wooden building was sited in no fewer than three different locations up to 1932. The present church was designed by Gilbert Fraser and built by local Holyhead builder John Jones. Work began in 1930 and the church was completed in April 1932 at a cost of £3,750. It is set in a large plot with no burials. Inside it had a terrazzo and woodblock floor and a plastered vaulted ceiling. There is stained glass in the triple lancet east window of the chancel which was installed in 1940. It shows Biblical figures as well as the female St Ffraid. Some windows in the north and south walls also have stained glass. The church underwent some restoration and refurbishment in 1989 and more recently in 1998-99. It is now partly carpeted. A visitor to the church will notice a curious stone arch in the north wall of the chancel; this arch is also visible on the outside of the building. The arch was intended to be part of an organ chamber. A pipe organ (originally from Eaton Hall, Cheshire) was given to the church in 1931 but was too large to be accommodated. The organ chamber archway was sealed up, presumably as a temporary measure, but it remains so to the present day. The organ in question was given to St Cybi's Church, Holyhead, and St Cybi's old organ given to Llanrhuddlad Church. The small organ at Llanrhuddlad was given to St Ffraid's Church. St Ffraid's church eventually acquired a pipe organ in 1994. Today St Ffraid's is an attractive little church and a good example of a 20th century church which has been tastefully restored for the 21st century. [20]

Holyhead – *St Seiriol*
The church was situated in Porth y Felin Road opposite the secondary school. Grid Reference SH 244 827.
The church of St Seiriol was intended as a second church to serve the growing population of Holyhead as the result of construction

of the railway and the harbour. An appeal for funds was launched in 1853 and a sum of £2,500 was soon realised. William Owen Stanley MP gave £500 and the land was given by the Marquess of Anglesey. Work on the new church started in August 1853, the architect being Charles Verelst of Liverpool. The church was completed in 1854 at a total cost of £4,200. It was a fairly large church, having a tower with a slender spire, nave, chancel and aisles. It was surrounded by a large churchyard where a large number of burials have taken place. In the 1970s the tower became unsafe, and although attempts were made to raise sufficient funds for restoration, the costs became prohibitive. Consequently the beautiful church of St Seiriol was demolished in 1992. No trace of it now remains except the base where it once stood. The churchyard remains in the hands of the church, but the number of damaged graves suggests that vandalism is a problem. [21]

Holyhead – ***St Mary's Roman Catholic Church/***
Eglwys Babyddol y Santes Fair

This church is situated on a site between Market Street and Longford Road. Grid Reference SH 246 825.

There was a Catholic place of worship in Holyhead in the 1850s largely to serve the needs of itinerant workers involved in the construction of the breakwater, the harbour and other works. However, a permanent church was not built until 1860 when St Mary's Church in Market Street was completed. It could accommodate 150 worshippers. For the rest of the 19th century it remained the only Catholic church in Anglesey. In 1965 it was replaced by a new church, built at a cost of £50,000, with underfloor heating and seating for 880 worshippers. In 1992 the site was extended to include a hall, a library and other facilities. [22]

Llanallgo – ***St Gallgo***

Llanallgo church is situated on the A5025 a short distance north of the Llanallgo roundabout. Grid Reference SH 501 851.

St Gallgo and his brothers St Gildas and St Eugrad were the sons of King Caw of Pictland. St Gallgo founded the church early in the

6th century and is one of the oldest Christian sites in Anglesey. It was mentioned in the Norwich Taxation documents of 1253. Originally Llanallgo was a chapel of ease to Llaneugrad church and before restoration in 1831 it dated back to the 14th or 15th century. The 1831 restoration included a new west window. Further reconstruction took place in 1892 including lengthening the nave; a stone bearing this date is located underneath the window at the west end of the church. The sanctuary was restored in 1934 and the oak panelling is in memory of the Reverend Stephen Roose Hughes (see below); this area is separated from the rest of the church by a simple altar rail. The large bell-cote contains a 13th century bell bearing the inscription *Ave Maria gracia plena* (Hail Mary full of grace). Unusually it also bears the imprint of a penny from the reign of Edward I. The bell was restored in 2000 at a cost of £3000. It is one of the oldest church bells in the diocese of Bangor. The porch is located on the north side of the church and houses a particularly wide door. Near the door stands a circular stone font on a fairly large base. The Victorian stained glass in the east window of the chancel depicts Jesus walking on the waters of the Sea of Galilee. An unusual feature of the interior is that the walls are lined with bricks which have been painted. At the beginning of the 19th century a traveller remarked that the interior of Llanallgo church was 'most slovenly kept'; two hundred years later it is very caringly maintained. The slate roof is in excellent condition. Unfortunately considerable damage was caused to the vestry by a fire in 2004, but this was repaired within weeks. Some 140 victims of the Royal Charter tragedy off Moelfre (in October 1859) are buried in the churchyard where an obelisk commemorates the disaster. The Reverend Stephen Roose Hughes (1815-1862) who worked tirelessly for the victims of the tragedy and their families is also buried in there. His grave, surrounded by metal railings, has been restored in recent years. His life is celebrated annually at the church. Charles Dickens stayed in the rectory (at that time the house next to the church) while he vistited the area to write about the tragedy. In 2004 a memorial stone to Manus Boyle who died in the Royal Charter disaster was placed near the north porch by some of his descendants. Well-known local hero Richard Evans, the Coxswain of the famous Moelfre Lifeboat, is also buried in the churchyard. [23]

Llanbabo – *St Pabo*

This church is situated on a minor road between Llanddeusant and Rhosgoch. Grid Reference SH 378 867.

This is a very ancient and historic church standing at the roadside near a stream; it was founded by St Pabo (who is believed to have been a king) in the 5th century and was once a chapel of ease to Llanddeusant. Pabo is often described as 'Pabo Post Prydain', Pabo the Pillar of Britain. A simple gate, looking very new but bearing the date 1836, leads into an oval churchyard. In fact the previous gate was stolen in 2004 and the present gate is a replica made by a local craftsman. The church, which is undivided into nave and chancel, has not suffered from excessive restoration. It is believed that most of the west, north and south walls are from the 12th century. Above the south door are carved chevron stones and carved human heads, probably from the 12th century. The bell-cote houses one bell, probably from the 18th century. The east window was rebuilt in the 14th century. Some restoration work (under architect Harold Hughes) took place in 1909. The windows contain unusual green glass; some of them have wooden frames. The roof timbers are medieval with more modern additions. The church has a simple wooden altar, the sanctuary being separated from the rest of the church by a wooden altar rail. There is a small harmonium and the worshippers sit on simple pews. The font is a circular bowl only about one foot high. Set against the north wall inside the church is a rectangular stone bearing a carving of the bearded King Pabo; this was discovered in the churchyard in the 17th century. The stone itself is thought to be from the 14th century and was probably intended to be used as an altar. It may have been thrown out of the church at the time of the Reformation. Inside the church above the south doorway is carved head, similar to those outside the church. Inside the church is a stone, formerly set in the churchyard wall, known as 'Diafol Llanbabo' (The Llanbabo Devil); it is thought that this represents a Celtic God. The church is no longer used on a regular basis but services are conducted here a few times every year. [24]

Llanbadrig – *St Padrig (old church)*

St Padrig's church is situated about a mile from the village of Cemaes. It is situated at the end of a minor road which leads off the A5025. Grid Reference SH 376 947.

Llanbadrig church is situated in a spectacular coastal cliff-top location. It has the distinction of being the most northerly place of worship in Wales. St Patrick (the patron saint of Ireland) is said to have been shipwrecked in 440 AD on the tiny island of Ynys Badrig (Middle Mouse) from where he managed to reach the Anglesey mainland. He founded his church near this point. Some believe it to be the first church dedicated to St Patrick; it is certainly one of the earliest churches to be established in Anglesey. At one time it would have been a royal chapel associated with the Llys of Cemaes. A fairly recently-built lychgate with a new sturdy wooden gate (and disabled access) leads into the exposed churchyard. The 14th century bell-cote contains one bell. Old gravestones from the late 17th century have been placed on either side of the large south porch. Originally the church was probably undivided into nave and chancel, but the chancel arch dates from the 14th century. The chancel, which is unusually long, is partly built into a quarried outcrop. The east window of the chancel dates from the 15th or 16th century. The church underwent repair and restoration work in 1812 (when the nearby house of Tyn Llan was built), and again in 1840 and 1884. The 1884 restoration was funded by Henry Edward John Stanley, third Baron Stanley of Alderley who had converted to Islam. The £800 restoration project was conditional on the incorporation of Islamic features, particularly the stained-glass windows and the blue tiles around the sanctuary. These tiles were specially made for Llanbadrig church. During this restoration a carved stone pillar 1.5m high and made of unusual black crystalline rock was discovered on the site. This stone, known as an Ichthus stone, is believed to date from the 9th century and bears fish and palm tree symbols. It is now inside the church in the west end. The church also contains a gravestone bearing a crudely-carved wheel-cross above a simple linear cross. The cylindrical font, about 16 inches high, is believed to date from the 12th century. In 1985, the church was badly damaged by fire

Parish Church of St.Mary and St Nicholas, Beaumaris.

Roman Catholig Church Amlwch.

Siwan's Tomb and Watchman's hut, Beaumaris Parish Church.

Roman Catholic Church, Beaumaris.

St Ceinwen's Church, Cerrigceinwen.

St Cybi's Church, Holyhead.

St Mary's Roman Catholic Church, Holyhead.

Stained glass window St Gallgo's Church, Llangallo.

St Mary's Church, Llanfairynghornwy.

St Patrick's Church, Llanbadrig.

Church of St Marcellus and St Marcellinus, Llanddeusant.

St Tysilio's Church, Menai Bridge.

The ruins of St Dwynwen's Church, Llanddwyn, showing the east wall of the chancel.

St Trygarn's Church, Llandrygarn.

St Tyfrydog's Church, Llandyfrydog.

St Machraeth's Church, Llanfachraeth.

St Maelog's Church, Llanfaelog.

St Maelog's Church, Llanfaelog. 12th century stone font housed in a modern base which also functions as a flower stand.

St Maethlu's Church, Llanfaethlu.

St Mary's Church, Llanfair Mathafarn Eithaf.

St Mary's Church, Llanfair Pwllgwyngyll.

Stained glass in east window of chancel, St Mary's Church, Llanfair Pwllgwyngyll.

St Mary's Church, Llanfair yn y Cwmwd.

Unusual cupola tower of St Mechell's Church, Llanfechell.

St Nidan's Church, Llanidan, near Brynsiencyn.

St Figel's Church, Llanfigel.

St Michael's Church, Llanfihangel Din Sylwy.

St Michael's Church, Llanfihangel Tre'r Beirdd.

St Cyngar's Church, Llangefni.

St Ceinwen's Church, Llangeinwen.

St Cawrdaf's Church, Llangoed.

St Cwyfan's Church, showing wall preventing erosion.

St Rhuddlad's Church, Llanrhuddlad is a landmark because of its tall spire.

Corbel stone, St Sadwrn's Church, Llansadwrn.

Church of St Afran, St Ieuan and St Sannan, Llantrisant. This church was built in 1899 and replaced the previous church.

St Gwenllwyfo's Church, Llanwenllwyfo.

East window of chancel, St Gwenllwyfo's Church, Llanwenllwyfo.

Stained glass in one of the south windows of the nave at St Gwenllwyfo's Church, Llanwenllwyfo.

St Credifael's Church, Penmynydd.

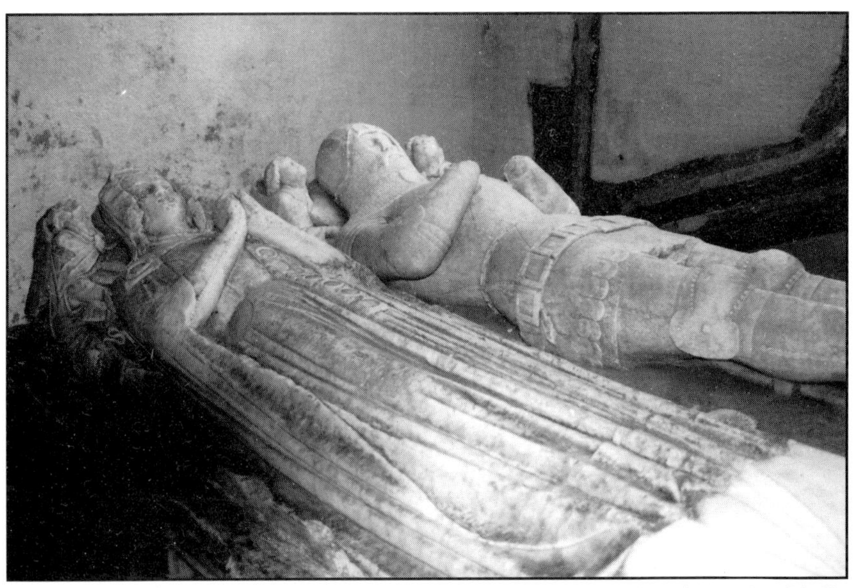

Alabaster Tomb of Gronw Tudur and his wife Myfanwy in north chapel at St Credifael's Church, Penmynydd.

Dog Tongs at St Credifael's Church, Penmynydd.

Stained glass in east window of chancel St Credifael's Church, Penmynydd.

Stained glass in north chapel (Tudor chapel) at St Credifael's Church, Penmynydd.

St Seiriol's Church, Penmon.

Cross in south Transept, St Seiriol's Church, Penmon.

Cross from Deer Park in nave at St Seiriol's Church, Penmon.

Hen Gapel Lligwy.

St Ceidio's Church, Rhodogeidio.

St Peirio's Church, Rhosbeirio, now disused.

St Gwenfaen's Church, Rhoscolyn.

but was reopened two years later after restoration said to cost £15,000. St Patrick's church contains a number of interesting and unusual features and these together with its superb location make it well worth seeing. [25]

Llanbadrig – *St Padrig, Cemaes (new church)*

This church stands in Cemaes near the roundabout on the west side of the village. Grid Reference SH 369 932.

The old parish church (see Llanbadrig) was some distance outside the village. This church, completed in 1865, was built of Anglesey limestone to an Early English design by Henry Kennedy and was intended to serve the village of Cemaes. It stands on a small plot with no gravestones, burials having continued in the churchyard of the old church. It is divided into nave and chancel, the former being particularly long. It has an ornate bell cote containing one bell. Most of the windows contain frosted leaded glass but one window of the south wall of the nave contains stained glass. There is only one small window in the south wall of the chancel, although the stonework suggests that more might have been intended. Behind the church is an annexe or meeting room. [26]

Llanbedrgoch – *St Peter/Sant Pedr*

The church is situated at the end of a narrow lane about half a mile west of the A5025 near the village of Llanbedrgoch.
Grid Reference SH 509 798.

Llanbedrgoch was once known as Llanfeistr. The church stands on raised ground. A simple lychgate leads to the churchyard. The church is cruciform in shape with the nave and chancel dating from the 15th century and the transepts from the 17th century. The church was restored in 1840 and 1885. The bell-cote contains one bell. Set into the wall on either side of the north doorway is a carved human face. The nave also had a south door which has been replaced by a window. The windows are all made of an unusual patterned glass some of which is coloured. Inside is an unusual desk made from benches from Llaneilian church. It is carved with the image of a mermaid holding a mirror and comb. The font is an octagonal bowl of unknown date. [27]

Llanbeulan – *St Peulan*

The church of St Peulan is about 0.7 mile (1.1 km) south of the A5 and also south of the A55, to the west of the village of Gwalchmai. Grid Reference SH 373 754.

The church of St Peulan was founded in 630 AD. St Peulan was the brother of St Gwenfaen of Rhoscolyn. An overgrown track leads to the church which is about 200 metres from the road. A small gate leads to the churchyard. The church is now redundant and was acquired by the Friends of Friendless Churches in 2004; some restoration work has since been undertaken. The large bell-cote contains one bell. The nave may date back as far as the 12th century. The chancel, the chancel arch and the south chapel are probably 14th century. The east window of the chancel is 15th century and the south window is 16th century. The windows of the nave are more recent. The nave also has a blocked doorway in the west wall but there is now no exterior evidence of this as the west wall has been rendered. The south chapel has a modern doorway in the east wall as well as a tiny reset 12th century window. Near the doorway is a stone bearing the inscription 1637 I.G. PEJ. The south window of the chapel is from the 17th century. None of the windows contains stained glass. The font is a rectangular bowl from the 11th/12th century, ornately decorated on three sides. A wooden panel which is part of a modern stall in the chancel bears the inscription *The seate of William Bold of Treyrddol, Esquire 1664.* The church is no longer used on a regular basis. [28]

Llanbeulan – *St Mary/Santes Fair, Talyllyn*

The church stands on the road between Aberffraw and Gwalchmai, about 2.5 miles (4.0 km) from Aberffraw. Grid Reference SH 367 729.

The church (now a Grade I listed building) stands in an exposed location in a sparsely populated area. It takes its name from Llyn Padrig which is a short distance to the south-west. At one time Talyllyn was one of the five chapels of ease belonging to Llanbeulan. Talyllyn is currently a part of the combined parish of Llanfaelog and Llangwyfan. A small gate leads into the churchyard which contains no gravestones. The present church was built in the 15th century. The chancel (with its arch) and the south chapel were added in the 16th or 17th century. The roof timbers are original and the roof slates are still in good order. All the windows, including the triple lancet of the chancel are of clear leaded glass. The exposed south side of the church has no windows. The door is on the west side and is deeply set into the wall, reflecting the thickness of its construction. The floor throughout the church is of flag stones. A small 12th century rectangular decorated font from Talyllyn is now housed in a modern stand at St Maelog's Church, Llanfaelog. In the nave at Talyllyn is a 15th century octagonal gritstone font. The seating is basic backless narrow plank pews. In fact many of these are modern copies since the originals were stolen in the 1990s when the church suffered vandalism. A simple painted wooden altar rail separates the sanctuary from the rest of the chancel. The south chapel no longer appears to be furnished. The church became redundant in 1992, but was acquired by the Friends of Friendless Churches in 1999 and they have undertaken some restoration work. Services are still occasionally held here in the summer months. [29]

Llanddaniel Fab – *St Deiniol*

This church stands, surrounded by houses, in the centre of the village. Grid Reference SH 496 704.

The small church of St Deiniol is the result of a complete rebuilding in the mid-19th century but parts of the nave may be older. It was further restored in 1873 by Henry Kennedy. There is a simple bell-cote at the west end and stained glass in the east window of the chancel and on the north side. Inside the church, above the vestry doorway, is a medieval, carved human face. Unfortunately no services have been conducted in the church for a few years and it now stands in disuse. The church is approached through an impressive slate-roofed lychgate leading to an overgrown path and an even more overgrown churchyard. The chancel is covered in ivy and a glance through the window reveals that cobwebs abound, although the pews and the organ are still in their place. [30]

Llanddeusant – *St Marcellus & St Marcellinus*

The church stands on the roadside in the village of Llanddeusant.
Grid Reference SH 346 853.

The church at Llanddeusant is dedicated to two saints, St Marcellus and St Marcellinus. Their names suggest they were not Celtic saints; it is believed that they may have been 4th century bishops from the Mediterranean area. The previous church underwent some restoration work in the early 19th century, but by the 1860s it was in poor condition and considered too small. A new church was completed in 1868; the architect was John Williams of Amlwch. It contained a decorated font, which came from the previous church. It was a circular bowl just over 2 feet tall and believed to be from the 12th century. Sadly the church became redundant in about 1994 but it was reopened in 2003 after being restored by the local community. A simple gateway leads into a very tidy churchyard. The church is divided into nave and chancel and has an impressive tower with a squat slated pyramidal top. The doorway is in the east wall of the tower. There is a vestry on the north side. Most of the windows contain frosted leaded glass, but the east window of the chancel contains stained glass. [31]

Llanddona – *St Dona*

The church is situated down a steep hill near the coast and about 1 mile (1.6 km) from the village of Llanddona.
Grid Reference SH 574 809

St Dona's church is believed to have been founded in 610 AD. The church was repaired in the 1840s and rebuilt completely in 1873 with the Rector, the Reverend Peter Jones, as architect. A simple lychgate (dated 1906) leads into the churchyard. On it is inscribed 'In loving memory of Henry Edward, Baron Stanley of Alderley, Patron and Benefactor of this church.' The present church, of cruciform design, has the font and south doorway from the previous church. A stone over the east window bearing the date 1566 has been placed in position upside-down. The bell-cote contains one bell which is dated 1647. There is stained glass in the east window of the chancel, but the other windows have an unusual opaque leaded glass. The 15th century church doorway in the south wall of the nave is decorated on both sides with various figures: a winged cherub, a human face, a dog and a bird. The font is a plain octagonal gritstone bowl of unknown date. [32]

Llanddwyn – *St Dwynwen* (see Newborough)

Llanddyfnan – *St Dyfnan*

The church is situated near the B5109 road about 2 miles (3.2 km) west of Pentraeth. Grid Reference SH 503 787.

A substantially built modern lychgate leads from a large car park into the churchyard. The nave and the annexe (on the west side) date from the 14th century. The chancel was rebuilt and widened in the 15th century and the south doorway was also added. The chancel arch is 14th century. In the annexe there are stairs leading to a gallery. The sturdy-looking bell-cote contains no bell. Above the south doorway is a carved human face surrounded by two hands below a drip-stone; it is believed to date from the 14th century. The church underwent extensive restoration in 1846-7. All the windows (including the east window of the chancel) are of plain leaded glass. On the north wall there is a memorial to those who died in the First World War. There is also a memorial to a father and son (Evan Rice Thomas and John Thomas) who served as churchwardens for many decades. The altar and altar cloth appear to be of some antiquity and behind is a simple wooden painted reredos. The grave of Richard Huws (1902-1980) of Talwrn, artist, designer and architect can be found in the churchyard. [33]

Llanddyfnan – *St Deiniol's Mission Church/ Eglwys Genhadol Sant Deiniol, Talwrn*

This church is located about 0.1 mile (0.2 km) south of the crossroads in the centre of Talwrn. Grid Reference SH 490 772.

This church was built to serve the village of Talwrn which is some distance from the parish churches of Llanddyfnan and Llanffinan. It stands at the centre of a fairly large plot; there are no burials around the church. It was built in 1891 on land donated by the Vivian family of Plas Gwyn, Pentraeth. The bell-cote contains one bell. The church is constructed of stone which has been pebble-dashed in parts. It is undivided into nave and chancel. Most of the windows contain clear glass, but the east window contains stained glass presented to the church in memory of Kathleen Elizabeth Anne Williams of nearby Plas Llanddyfnan. [34]

Llandegfan – *St Tegfan*

The church stands near a junction on the northern outskirts of the village of Llandegfan. Grid Reference SH 564 744.

The present church stands on the site of previous church buildings. The nave and chancel are on the original foundations but the north chapel and the transepts are newer. The tower of the present church was added during an 1811 restoration. An inscription on the tower (in Latin and in Welsh) commemorates the fact that it was built by the Honourable Thomas James Warren Bulkeley. The belfry contains a bell dated 1666. The castellated tower has a south-facing clock and a weather vane. The south porch contains a 14th century doorway. The extension to the north transept (the north chapel) was added early in the 19th century. There was general restoration work in 1901-03 under diocesan architect Peter S. Gregory. A font (probably from the 14th century) was discovered at the time of this restoration. It now stands in the churchyard between the porch and the transept and is currently a receptacle for a potted plant. The chancel and transepts have stained glass windows. In the churchyard is the grave of Thomas Williams (1737-1802). During his lifetime he was known as 'The Copper King' and 'Twm Chwarae Teg' (Tom Fair Play). He made his fortune from the copper mines of Mynydd Parys. [35]

Llandrygarn – *St Trygarn*

The church is at the end of a narrow lane which turns off the B5109 between Llynfaes and Bodedern. Grid Reference SH 383 796.

An simple lychgate leads from a small parking place into the well-maintained churchyard of St Trygarn's church. This small, tidy, rural church was renovated in 1841. In 1872 a further restoration saw the building of a new chancel and new windows were also fitted. The architect was Henry Kennedy. The bell-cote contains one bell. In the south wall of the chancel is a reset 13th century doorway; this was previously the north doorway of the nave. The south doorway of the nave is from the 15th century. The west window of the nave is from the 14th century and the easterly window on the south side of the nave is 14th/15th century. All other windows of the nave and chancel are modern. All the windows contain plain leaded glass; there is no stained glass. The roof of the nave is medieval. Some hold the view that there was no saint named Trygarn, and that the word simply refers to a geographical feature (trygarn = large cairn). [36]

Llandyfrydog – *St Tyfrydog*

The church is situated 1 mile (1.6 km) south of the village of Parc.
Grid Reference SH 443 853.

The church of St Tyfrydog stands in a wooded area near a quiet, winding country road. A church on this site was listed in the Norwich Taxation in 1254. The nave was probably built in the 14th century and the chancel was rebuilt about 1500 but retaining the chancel arch which dates from about 1400. The south porch and north vestry are modern additions. The bell-cote contains one bell. The east window of the chancel is 15th century and is the only one of the windows to contain stained glass. The nave formerly had a north doorway but this has been converted into a window. The south window of the nave is 15th century. The pews are painted a cream colour. The church underwent restoration in 1860-62 by Henry Kennedy and John Rogers (with construction of a new porch and vestry and two new windows) but retaining some early features. The interior underwent minor refurbishment in 1988. There is a brass sundial on a stone plinth in the churchyard, probably dating from the 18th century; it stands near the south porch but is not complete. The church is about 1 mile (1.6 km) north of Clorach, which according to legend was the meeting place of St Cybi and St Seiriol. [37]

Llandysilio – *St Mary/Santes Fair*

This church is located in Menai Bridge within yards of Telford's suspension bridge. Grid Reference SH 555 717.

By the 1850s the small island church of St Tysilio (see below) was inadequate for the growing Anglican congregation of Menai Bridge. The Rector (the Reverend Thomas Jones Williams, who was also the Rector of St Mary's church, Llanfair Pwllgwyngyll) wished to see the establishment of a new church closer to the town. The new church was built in an elevated position near to the Menai suspension bridge at a cost of £1,450, and was consecrated in 1858. Financial support was given by the Marquess of Anglesey. It was designed by Henry Kennedy as a simple Gothic style church with no stained glass or organ. Both these features were later additions. The church walls incorporate a number of buttresses. One of the church's most notable features is the ornate tower at the west end which contains a belfry and a clock with one face, facing west. There is no cemetery surrounding the church; this is because burials continued in the churchyard of the old church of St Tysilio on Church Island. A programme of refurbishment including the provision of an upper floor began in 2006. [38]

Llandysilio – *St Tysilio*

The church can be reached by walking through a wooded area known as Coed Cyrnol and crossing the causeway leading to the island. Unless there is an exceptionally high tide, access is always possible.
Grid Reference SH 552 717.

St Tysilio was the son of King Brochmael of Powys and a grandson of St Pabo (see Llanbabo). He founded his cell about 630 AD on the small island where the present church stands. The present tiny church (undivided into nave and chancel) dates from the 14th or 15th century and some of its original features remain. Later restoration has taken place, particularly in the 1890s. The east window dates from this period (1897) and is a reproduction of the 15th century original. The windows in the north and south sides are of plain coloured glass. There is no window in the west side, but there is a simple bell-cote containing one bell. A strange feature is the rectangular door surrounded by a massive pointed door frame. Inside the church, which has whitewashed walls, there is a plain stone altar. A simple wooden screen separates the sanctuary from the rest of the church where there are wooden pews. The roof beams are thought to be medieval. The octagonal font dates from the 14th century. The church contains an organ and is lit by three candelabras suspended from the roof. It has a stone floor, some of which are inscribed gravestones. The church of St Tysilio was at one time a chapel of ease to St Mary's Church, Llanfair Pwllgwyngyll. The rector of St Mary's was instrumental in building the new church in Menai Bridge, as a replacement for St Tysilio's island church which had become too small in the 1850s. The church is at one corner of a large churchyard where, unusually, the graves are arranged in a radial pattern, i.e. not all the graves are aligned east-west as is the normal custom in Christian burials. At the highest point of the churchyard is a war memorial for those from Menai Bridge who lost their lives in two World Wars. The famous Welsh poet Cynan (Albert Evans), who lived in Menai Bridge for many years, is buried on the island. No new graves have been opened here for some years; the town now uses a new cemetery near Holyhead Road. [39]

Llanedwen – *St Edwen/Santes Edwen*

The church is situated about 1 mile (1.6 km) down a lane leading off the A4080 about 2 miles (3.2 km) south of Llanfair Pwllgwyngyll.

Grid Reference SH 517 683.

St Edwen founded her cell in this tranquil spot in 640 AD. The present church was designed by Henry Kennedy and built in 1856, incorporating some masonry from the previous building in the lower part of the west wall. Repairs were undertaken in 1956. Its tower and spire make it a landmark visible from a considerable distance, even from the mainland. An unusual feature is that the tower wall has slates on part of the south side. Inside the church are numerous memorials from the 17th and 18th centuries; the earliest (to Thomas Owen, Bolydon) is dated 1646. There are three 17th century chairs, a 19th century reading desk incorporating some 14th century features, and a pulpit containing a 17th century carved frieze. There is also a pair of oak dog tongs which are from the 19th century. The church has always had close links with the nearby Plas Newydd estate and some of the Marquesses of Anglesey are buried in the churchyard, as are many of their former employees. Local cleric and historian Henry Rowlands (1655-1723) (author of *Mona Antiqua Restaurata*, published in 1723) is also buried here, as is William Bulkeley Hughes (1797-1882) of Plas Coch, landowner and High Sheriff of Anglesey in 1861. Llanedwen church has the distinction of being the only church in Wales in regular use to be lit entirely by candles. It is also interesting to note that the only liturgy used at Llanedwen is the 1662 Book of Common Prayer. St Edwen's church is little changed since it was built; it is a good example of an unspoilt 19th century country church. [40]

Llaneilian – *St Eilian*

The church is situated on a minor road about 1.5 miles (2.4 km) from the village of Penysarn. Grid Reference SH 470 929.

This church is very different in appearance from most Anglesey churches and is a well-preserved example of a medieval church (Figure 8). St Eilian established this early 'clas' church in the 5th/6th century. According to legend St Eilian was sent by the Pope as an emissary to Cadwallon Lawhir in the 5th century; with him he brought some oxen. The greedy Cadwallon seized the oxen and was struck blind by St Eilian as a punishment. In return for restoring his sight, Cadwallon gave St Eilian as much land as a deer could cover while being pursued by his hounds; this became the land on which St Eilian established his cell. Two different lychgates lead to the churchyard. The Norman tower of the present church dates from the 12th century and has recently been painted white. The spire above the tower has an unusual pyramidal shape. A stone stairway provides access to the tower which contains three bells, the earliest dated 1638. The nave and chancel are believed to have been rebuilt in the late 15th century; the south porch is of about the same period. The east window of the chancel is from the 15th century; it contains stained glass. The church underwent repairs in 1929, the architects being Harold

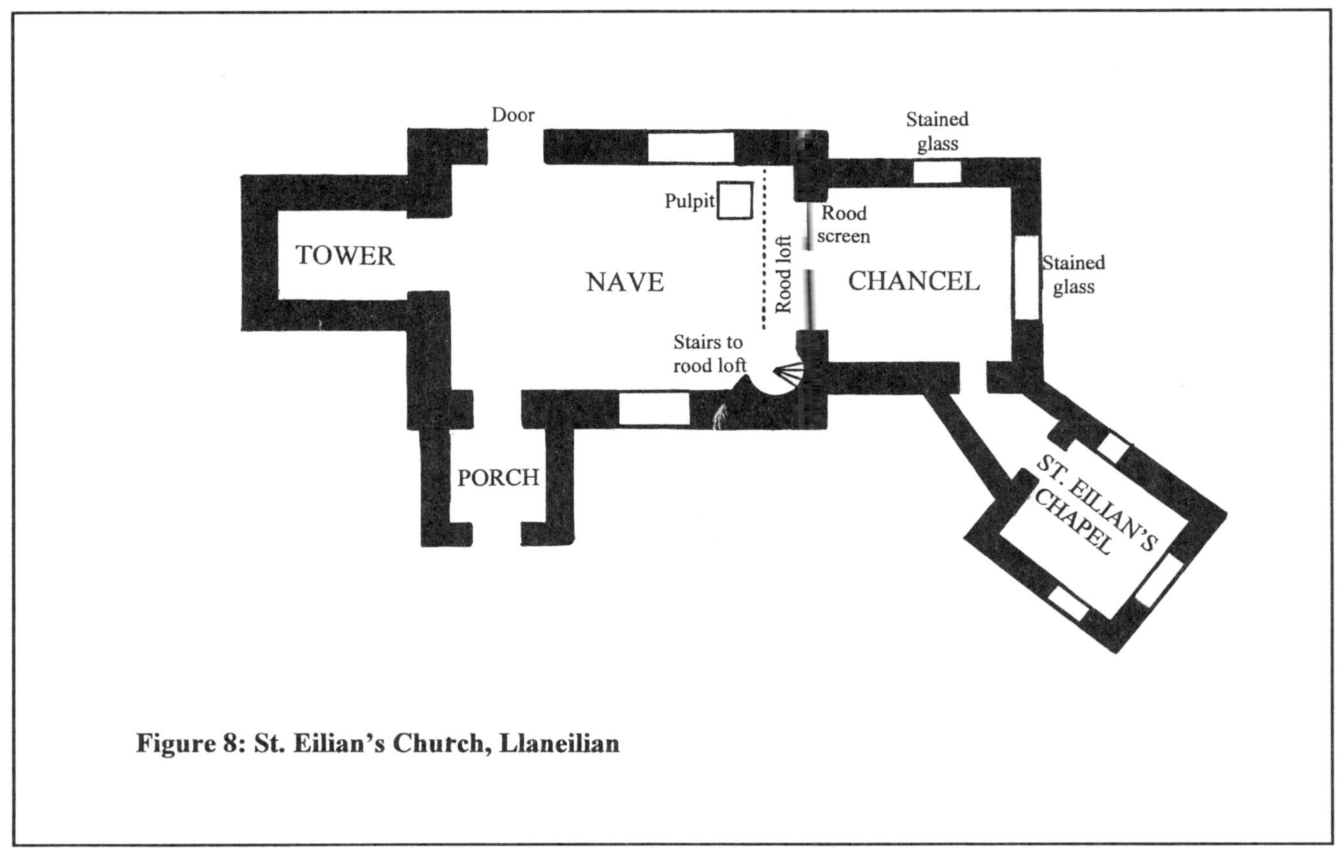

Figure 8: St. Eilian's Church, Llaneilian

Hughes and William Griffith Williams. The 15th century oak rood screen is magnificently carved and a painted figure of Death as a skeleton probably dates from the 16th century. The painting bears the inscription 'Colyn Angau yw Pechod' (*Sin is the Sting of Death*). In the nave is a portrait of St Eilian thought to be from the late 17th or early 18th century. In the south-east corner of the nave is a circular stair to the rood-loft. The altar is from the 17th century. Outside, the elaborate architecture is a reflection of the church's wealth which derived from pilgrims visiting Ffynnon Eilian (St Eilian's Well) 500m north west of the church on a cliff top near the sea shore (SH 466 934). An oak chest bound by metal straps and studded with nails, known as Cyff Eilian (dated 1667), is said to have held their donations. This chest can be seen inside the church as well as dog-tongs (dated 1748) used to separate quarrelsome dogs in church. The communion table incorporates a panel dated 1634. The side chapel (St Eilian's Chapel) is situated to the south-east of the church; it dates from the late 14th century and may be the site of St Eilian's original cell. It is set at an angle and linked to the church by a passage (built in 1614). The exterior wall of the passage contains a stone bearing the inscription RPR WK RH 1614. The churches at Coedana, Rhosbeirio and Bodewryd were once chapels of ease to Llaneilian. The unusual nature of Llaneilian church make it essential viewing. [41]

Llaneugrad – *St Eugrad*

The church is situated at the end of a narrow wooded lane which leads off the B5110 about 0.5 mile (0.8 km) south of Marianglas.
Grid Reference SH 496 842.

This small church is situated near the site of a 4th century hill fort on the Parciau estate. A lychgate leads directly to the church door, but there is also a separate entrance to the churchyard. Most of the walls (except those of the porch and north chapel) are covered in a cement render. The church is divided into nave and chancel (from the 12th century), both having considerable headroom. The chancel arch is also 12th century. The north chapel was added in the 16th century. A very large beam separates the chancel from the chapel which has a blocked doorway in the west wall. The south doorway is from the 15th century. The vestry on the north side is a more modern addition, as is the south porch which is unusual in that it has a flat roof with castellation. The bell-cote contains one bell. All the windows contain clear leaded glass; there is no stained glass. Inside the church in a recess in the north wall of the nave is a stone crucifix from the 13th century. It shows a figure on a wheel cross with pierced spandrels. The font is a plain bowl about 15 inches high. [42]

Llanfachraeth – *St Machraeth*

The church is situated near the A5025 at the north end of the village. Grid Reference SH 314 827.

A small gate leads into the churchyard. The church was entirely rebuilt in about 1878, but it contains several memorials from the old church. The bell-cote contains one bell. In the west wall are two stones with crudely carved human faces; one is below the bell-cote, the other near the southern end of the wall. Both stones are much weathered. Inside the church there are three panels from a 17th century pew bearing a coat of arms; one is dated 1626. Most of the windows contain frosted leaded glass, but there is stained glass in the nave and in the east window of the chancel which is in three lights. The font is a circular bowl of uncertain date. [43]

Llanfaelog – *St Maelog*

The church is situated on the A4080 in the village of Llanfaelog, just opposite the Post Office. Grid Reference SH 337 730.

St Maelog's church was founded about 605 AD. Llanfaelog was once one of five chapels of ease belonging to Llanbeulan. The present church was designed by architects Henry Kennedy and Richard Kyrke Penson and completed in 1848. It is interesting to note that funding came from the Chester and Holyhead Railway who built the railway to Holyhead in the late 1840s over land belonging to the church. A bell-cote on the west side of the church is decorated with a Celtic cross; it houses one bell. Access to the church is through a heavy gate mounted on sturdy gateposts. A sloping path leads to the modern glass porch door on the south side, and gives easy access for the disabled. The church underwent extensive modernisation in 2001, to a design by architect Adam Voelcker. The refurbishment also included the construction of an entrance hall and a gallery (the Juniper Gallery) with new roof windows on the north and south sides, as well as toilets and a kitchen. Impressive etched glass doors (produced by Bill Swann of Porthmadog) provide access to the main part of the church; the doors, as well as a window in the gallery, have a 'Tree of Life' theme. The church has a high roof with beams painted grey and is carpeted throughout. In the north wall of the nave is a stained glass window depicting St Cecilia (the patron saint of music). This window is thought to be by Edward Burne-Jones; it commemorates John Price Roberts who died in 1857. Also in the north wall of the nave is a stained glass window in memory of the Reverend Robert Williams who was rector of the church for 38 years; he died in 1902. The stained glass in the west window (in the Juniper Gallery) depicts Saint Paul and is also dedicated to the Reverend Robert Williams. The stained glass in the east window of the chancel dates from 1881 and depicts the Last Supper. The 21st century stained glass 'music window' in the south wall is by Tiffany Tate. The font is a small 12th century rectangular stone font which came from St Mary's Church, Talyllyn and is now housed on a modern wooden base (also having the 'Tree of Life' theme) by local craftsman Colin Pearce. The nave altar, pulpit and altar rails are all modern and on the same theme. The carved altar and reredos directly underneath the east window date from 1937. Outside there are new paths through the neat churchyard where there are shipwreck graves, including a barrel mortuary in which bodies awaiting identification were stored. There are also graves for those who died in a 1941 aircraft accident at sea. At night the church is floodlit. This church has been carefully restored and is well maintained; it is a tasteful blend of the modern and the traditional and is well worth seeing. [44]

Llanfaelog – *Christ Church/Eglwys Crist, Rhosneigr*
This church is situated on the northern outskirts of Rhosneigr. Grid Reference SH 322 737.
This church does not resemble the majority of Anglesey churches – it could easily be mistaken for a village hall. It has a whitewashed exterior and a slate roof with red ridge tiles. There is a bell-cote on the east end. The windows are of plain leaded glass. Two stones on either side of the front porch (which faces west) suggest that the church dates from 1908. However, ordnance survey maps indicate that there was a mission room on the site in the 1890s. The church is in disuse since about 1995 and is currently in poor condition with crumbling exterior plasterwork and loose slates. It is now in private hands. [45]

Llanfaes – *St Catherine*
The church is situated on a minor road which leads off the B5109 about 1 mile (1.6 km) north of Beaumaris. Grid Reference SH 605 779.
The name Llanfaes means 'church on flat open ground'. Llywelyn ap Iorwerth (Llywelyn Fawr) founded a Franciscan monastery here. His wife Siwan (or Joan), daughter of King John of England, was buried here in 1237, as was Llywelyn's mother Serena in 1263. When Henry IV brought soldiers to Anglesey to defeat Owain Glyndŵr, the monastery was partly destroyed because the monks supported Glyndŵr. Although the monastery was subsequently rebuilt, it did not survive the Dissolution of the Monasteries in the 1530s. The Friary church was still standing in the 18th century but was demolished in the 19th century after being used as a barn. At one time the church of St Catherine was the richest in Anglesey. It was restored in 1811-12 by Lord Bulkeley when the impressive tower was added. In 1845 the nave and chancel were rebuilt and a spire added to the tower; the architect was Matthew Hadfield. Later additions in the 19th century were the side chapels built by two local landowning families: the Bulkeleys (of Baron Hill) and the Hamptons (of Henllys Hall). The south aisle was added in 1890 by diocesan architect Henry Kennedy. There are stained glass windows in the chancel and the chapels. The north side of the churchyard contains an ornate memorial marking the grave of

John Elias (1774-1841) the famous Welsh Nonconformist preacher. His funeral is said to have been one of the largest ever seen in Anglesey. Buried here too are John Williams and Llywelyn Lloyd, both famous preachers. Also buried here are Owen Owen and his two sisters who died in the tragic 'Rothesay Castle' shipwreck in 1831. Set into the south wall of the church is a stone commemorating two burials in 1720. A stone showing a Latin cross within a circle is set into the east gable; it is medieval. On the eastern boundary of the churchyard is a sombre-looking mausoleum for the Hampton-Lewis family of nearby Henllys Hall. [46]

Llanfaethlu – ***St Maethlu***

The church is situated at the centre of the village.
Grid Reference SH 313 871.

A small gateway leads into the sloping churchyard; the church itself overlooks the surrounding open countryside. The nave of the present church is the original 15th century church; the south porch is believed to be from around the same period. The roof of the nave and porch are slated with large crudely-made slates. The windows in the north and south walls of the nave are from the 17th and 15th centuries respectively. The roof timbers of the nave are obscured by a ceiling. The chancel and some new windows were added in 1874, the architect being Henry Kennedy. In the east wall is set a 15th century window containing unusual patterned opaque glass with orange glass edges. The bell-cote contains one bell, dated 1760. The font is an octagonal bowl which dates from 1640. In the nave is a large high backed pew made from an original 17th century box-pew. Near the south wall there are a number of gravestones from the 17th and 18th centuries. [47]

Llanfair Mathafarn Eithaf – ***St Mary/Santes Fair***

The church is situated on a minor road which leads off the B5108 1 mile (1.6 km) west of Benllech. Grid Reference SH 507 829.

A small gate leads to the churchyard which occupies a considerable area on the north side. The church is of medieval origin with a 15th century nave. This nave probably represents the original church, the chancel being a 15th century addition. In 1848 the church underwent a restoration by diocesan architect Henry Kennedy, and the nave windows, bell gable and vestry date from that period. The bell-cote contains one bell dated 1849 but which looks very new. The porch is on the south side (containing a 16th century doorway) but there is also a doorway (14th century) in the north wall. All the windows are of plain leaded glass. There is a gallery on the west side. This church is associated with the famous Welsh poet Goronwy Owen. He was born nearby in 1723 and was a curate here for a period of three weeks in 1746 before he lost the job to a more favoured candidate. Later, he left Wales never to return. He became a curate in various places in England before emigrating to the United States where he became head of a theological college in Virginia. He died there in 1769. [48]

Llanfair Mathafarn Eithaf – *St Andrew's Church/ Eglwys Sant Andreas, Benllech*

This church is situated in the centre of the village on the A5025 road, opposite a shopping precinct. Grid Reference SH 518 827.

This church was completed in July 1964 and was built to serve the growing community of Benllech. It is next to a church hall built some decades previously. The church is of modern design with large plain glass windows and a high roof. It is undivided into nave and chancel. The altar is on a raised area, being divided from the rest of the church by a simple altar rail. Behind the altar is a large cross on the east wall. Next to the west wall (which is almost entirely of glass) is a large font of grey stone. The church has no pews but individual chairs allowing greater flexibility of use. [49]

Llanfair Mathafarn Eithaf – *St Andrew's Mission Church/Eglwys Genhadol Sant Andreas*

This church is situated 1 mile (1.6 km) south west of the village of Brynteg on the B5110. Grid Reference SH 486 813.

This mission church was built in the late 19th century in this sparsely populated area. It became redundant in the 1960s and was unused for some years before being converted into a house. The bell-cote is still in place but without its bell. The building has subsequently been extended but its ecclesiastical origins are still apparent. [50]

Llanfair Pwllgwyngyll – *St Mary/Santes Fair*

The church stands at the end of a narrow lane about 0.2 mile (0.3 km) south of the main A5 road on the east side of the village of Llanfair Pwllgwyngyll. Grid Reference SH 537 713.

The earliest religious cell on this site probably dates from the 7th century. It is interesting to note that the island church of St Tysilio (in Menai Bridge) was once a chapel of ease belonging to St Mary's church, Llanfair Pwllgwyngyll. A medieval church stood on this magnificent site on the shore of the Menai Straits before the present church was built; it was demolished in 1852. It was unusual amongst Anglesey churches in that the east wall of the chancel had an apse. A completely new church, designed by Henry Kennedy, was completed in 1853 at a cost of £950 (Figure 9). The catalyst for the building of the new church was the then Rector, the Reverend Thomas Jones Williams M.A. (whose grave can be seen in the churchyard below the east window of the chancel). Llanfair Pwllgwyngyll had grown in importance as a result of Telford's A5 road, the coming of the railway and the construction of the Britannia Bridge and the Reverend Williams believed the parish deserved a better and larger church. The new church was consecrated by the Bishop of Bangor on 7 September, 1853. Entrance to the churchyard is through an impressive lychgate which bears the Greek letters alpha and omega. At the south-west end of the church is a tower (incorporating a belfry) on which stands an impressive slender spire. At the four corners of the base of the spire are carved stone animals. The church door is incorporated into the tower. The walls of the church and the tower are strengthened by impressive buttresses. The slate roof is very steeply pitched. A small vestry with its own doorway at the east end of the church was added in the 1880s. The stained glass window in the east wall depicts various Biblical scenes and is dedicated to the memory of the first Marquess of Anglesey and is dated 1876. High in the west wall is a stained glass window dedicated to Sir Robert Waller Otway; it was installed in 1876. The

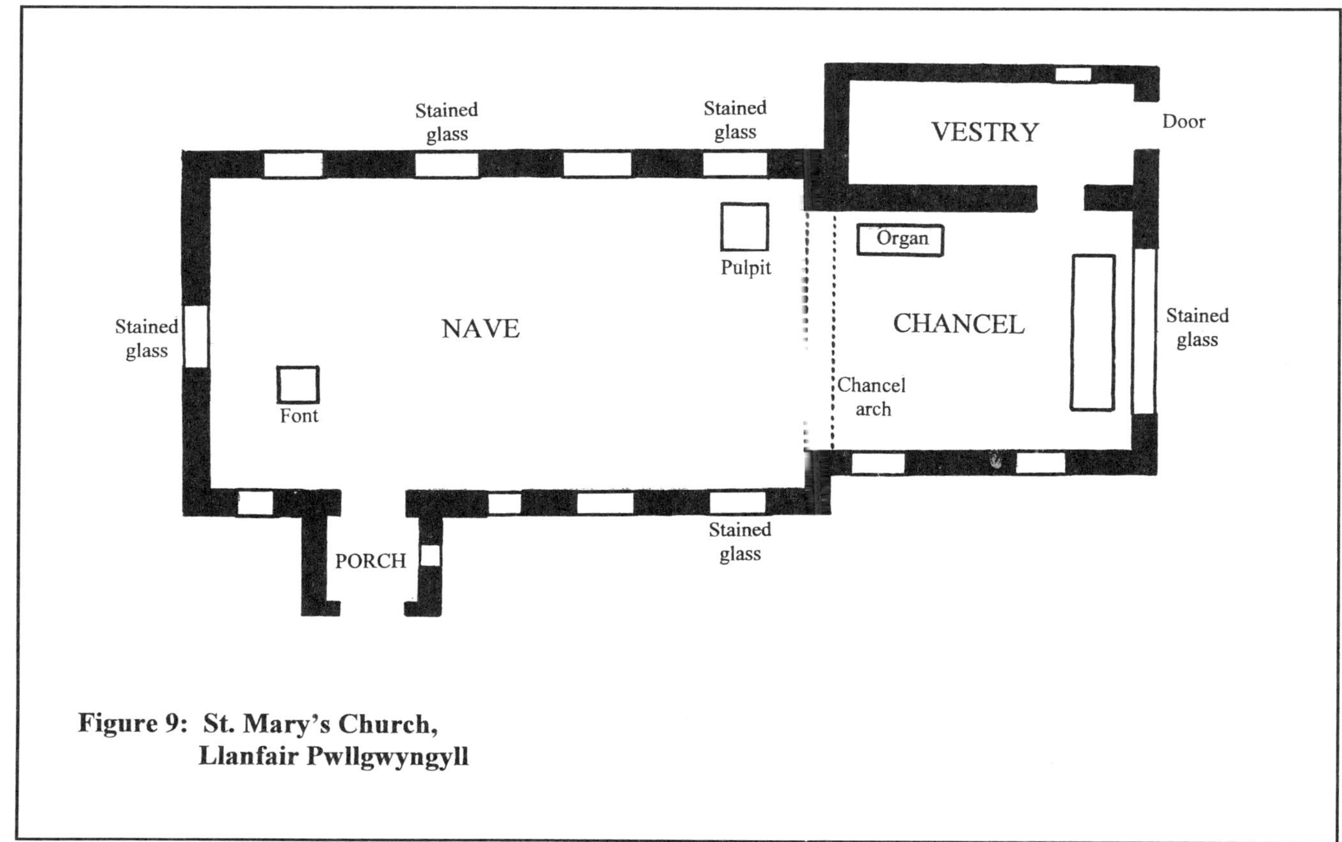

Figure 9: St. Mary's Church, Llanfair Pwllgwyngyll

stained glass window in the south wall of the nave and the brass lectern are dedicated to the memory of Harry Clegg of nearby Plas Llanfair. The reredos and pulpit are of granite and both date from 1901. They commemorate members of the Morgan family of nearby Plas Coed Môr as does one of the stained glass windows in the north wall of the nave. A more modern stained glass window in the north wall of the nave commemorates the work of the Indefatigable Nautical Training School which was located nearby from 1864 until its closure in 1995. A tablet on the north wall of the nave is in memory of those who died in the First World War; the simple wooden altar rail is dedicated to those who died in the Second World War. The church contains some artefacts from Uganda; this is because it has formed an association with an Ugandan parish. The roof timbers of the chancel are hidden by unusual wood panelling. The octagonal font is the same age as the church and it must be presumed, therefore, that the font from the old church was destroyed or lost at the time of its demolition. The wooden conical shaped font cover dates from 1955. Around the church is an uneven churchyard with a few yew trees and a tiny stream flows through it. The churchyard contains a memorial to those who lost their lives in the construction of the Britannia Bridge in the 19th century and its subsequent reconstruction in the 1970s. A total of twenty names are inscribed on this memorial. In the churchyard can be seen the grave of Sir John Morris Jones (1864-1929), the distinguished Welsh academic who was Professor of Welsh at the University of Wales, Bangor from 1895. The grave is marked by an impressive Celtic cross near the highest part of the churchyard. In the south side of the churchyard on the path leading down to the Straits stands an intricately carved Celtic cross surrounded by four small yew trees. This commemorates members of the Clegg family of Plas Llanfair. Looking towards the Menai Straits from the churchyard it is possible to see a statue of Horatio Nelson, erected in 1873. [51]

Llanfairynghornwy – *St Mary/Santes Fair*

The church is situated on a minor road 1 mile (1.6 km) north-west of the A5025. Grid Reference SH 327 908.

Although it is dedicated to the scriptural saint Mary, some believe that the church may have been established by a Celtic saint named Pedyr Lanuaur. A short path leads to the impressive lychgate. St Mary's church is a fairly large church of medieval appearance, standing in a quiet wooded location. The former rectory stands nearby. At one time St Mary's church was a chapel of ease to Llanddeusant church. The walls of the nave and the chancel arch are from the 11th or 12th century. The windows in the north and south walls of the nave are from the 16th and 14th centuries respectively. The chancel underwent rebuilding and lengthening in the 15th century; its east window is from this period. The south chapel and the arcade (of three arches) were completed in the late 15th or early 16th century and the chapel's east window is from this period. The tower was added in the 17th century; it is topped a squat pyramidal structure. The bell-cote is incorporated into the west wall of the tower; it contains a 17th century bell. The church door is also in the west wall of the tower; the original south porch is now used as a vestry. There is stained glass in the east window of the chancel; there is also patterned stained glass in the north wall of the nave. Restoration work financed by Richard Lloyd of Rhosbeirio took place in 1812. The church underwent further restoration in 1847 under architects John Weightman and Matthew Hadfield, and in 1860 another restoration was carried out under the direction of the Rector, the Reverend James Williams. Restoration of the chancel and chapel was undertaken in the 1930s. Inside the church is a memorial to Evan Thomas (1735-1814), the founder of the famous Anglesey family of bone-setters, who is buried in the churchyard. Also buried there are the Reverend James Williams (1790-1872) and his wife Frances (1797-1858). They arrived in Llanfairynghornwy at about the time that a ship called the *Alert* sank in a violent storm with the loss of 140 lives. They established the Anglesey Association for the Preservation of Lives from Shipwreck in 1828, later to become a part of the RNLI. James Williams was Rector at Llanfairynghornwy from 1821 until 1872; his father John Williams was Rector before him for 53 years. [52]

Llanfair yn Neubwll – *St Mary/Santes Fair*

The church is situated near a farm on a minor road 0.8 mile (1.4 km) south-east of Valley. Grid Reference SH 297 778.

The church stands within a walled enclosure in an isolated location near the main Holyhead railway line. It is also fairly near two lakes, Llyn Penrhyn and Llyn Dinam, from which it derives its name. A short walk across a field leads to the churchyard. The church is essentially a 14th century structure undivided between nave and chancel. The bell-cote contains one bell. The doorway is in the north wall. The east window is 14th century and the easterly window in the north wall is 15th century; the other windows are more recent and were inserted in the 1857 restoration by Henry Kennedy. The roof was reslated and some roof timbers were replaced in this restoration but some medieval roof trusses still remain. Inside the church the box pews were replaced by open pews. This restoration was apparently partly funded by the Chester and Holyhead Railway Company. The church was closed for regular worship in the mid-1970s, but the churchyard is still maintained. Services are still conducted here on a very occasional basis. The church had a 12th century circular gritstone font. This font was apparently taken to St Cybi's church, Holyhead for safekeeping. The grave of the Reverend Henry Rees, the noted preacher who died in 1908, is in the churchyard. He was the son of the poet William Rees, better known as *Gwilym Hiraethog*. [53]

Llanfair yn y Cwmwd – *St Mary/Santes Fair*

The church is situated 0.9 mile (1.5 km) north of Llangeinwen church near Dwyran. A tiny well-hidden lane on the left leads to the church which stands about 100 yards from the road. Grid Reference SH 447 667.

The parish of Llanfair yn y Cwmwd was occasionally referred to as Llanfair Fach on account of its small size. The church stands in a small clearing surrounded by a well-maintained churchyard. There are comparatively few gravestones on the south side of the churchyard. The walls of the present church are thought to be medieval, but the church has undergone restoration at various times including in 1936 when repairs were carried out, the architects being Harold Hughes and William G. Williams. The church door is on the north side. There is a small oval shaped 12th century decorated font with a wooden cover. An ornately-carved 13th century coffin lid is set against the north wall of the chancel. The bell-cote houses one bell which is dated 1582. Inside the church a simple wooden rood screen separates the nave and chancel. In the east part of the churchyard is the grave of Maurice Wilks (1904-1963), inventor of the Land Rover. Wilks had some connection with this part of Anglesey and early prototypes of this famous vehicle were tested in the area. The church is a good example of a small unspoilt country church. [54]

Llanfechell – *St Mechell*

The church stands in a prominent position in the village square.
Grid Reference SH 369 913.

This unusual white-washed cruciform church stands among yew trees in a circular walled churchyard in the quiet picturesque village of Llanfechell. The nave and the western part of the chancel date from the 12th century and the chancel lengthened in the 13th century. The south transept was built in the 14th century, but the north transept is of uncertain date. Impressive arches separate the transepts from the rest of the church. The south porch is believed to be medieval. The square tower on the west side was built in the 16th century and has an unusual 18th century cupola (bee-hive shaped) spire, the only one of its type in Anglesey. There is a late 13th century gravestone in the porch. There is stained glass in the chancel and the south transept. The church underwent restoration in 1840 and 1870 when alterations were made to the north transept. There is a medieval carved stone showing a human face above the stained glass window of the south transept. The font is a square gritstone block from the 12th century. The church contains a silver gilt cup, manufactured in Germany in 1583, which has been in Anglesey since 1686. It is said that the 18th century diarist, William Bulkeley (1691-1760) of the nearby mansion of Brynddu, gave orders that the church bell be silenced because it turned his beer sour! William Bulkeley is buried in the churchyard. [55]

Llanfeirian – *St Meirian* (see Llangadwaladr)

Llanffinan – *St Ffinan*

The church is situated at the end of an unsurfaced lane which leads off the Talwrn to Ceint road. Grid Reference SH 496 755.

The churchyard is surrounded by a modern wall and an equally modern gate allows access to the well-maintained churchyard. The church is a good example of a small rural church, completely rebuilt in a Romanesque style in 1841, the architect being John Welch. Its style is quite different to most Anglesey churches. The bell-cote contains one bell and the church doorway is situated in the west wall. There are stained glass windows in the east wall of the chancel and small stained glass windows in the north and south walls. These windows were gifts in memory of local people. The font is a crudely decorated circular gritstone bowl thought to be from the 12th century. [56]

Llanfflewin – *St Fflewin*

The church is situated in an isolated spot about 1 mile (1.6 km) east of the village of Llanrhuddlad in an area known as Mynydd Mechell.
Grid Reference SH 349 891.

The religious cell was founded in 630 AD by St Fflewin. The church is undivided into nave and chancel. The church underwent some repair work in the early 19th century with further restoration in 1864. Reroofing and general restoration was undertaken in 1933-4 by architects Harold Hughes and William G. Williams. The church contains no features older than the 18th century. The font is an undecorated nine-sided bowl from the 14th/15th century. From 1859 to 1874 the Rector of Llanfflewin (as well as nearby Llanrhuddlad) was the well-known poet and literary figure the Reverend Morris Williams MA (better known by his bardic name *Nicander*); he won the chair at the National Eisteddfod in 1849. St Fflewin's church is a typical, well-preserved rural church and is well worth a visit. [57]

Llanfigail – ***St Figel***

The church is situated in a country lane about 1.5 miles (2.4 km) north of Bodedern. Grid Reference SH 328 828.

Llanfigail church was formerly a chapel of ease to nearby Llanfachraeth church and was listed in the Norwich Taxation of 1254. It is a tiny church, undivided into nave and chancel, standing in a small well-maintained plot. The roof slates are almost entirely hidden by cement. It had fallen into ruin by the 18th century and the famous Morris brothers (Morrisiaid Môn: Lewis, William and Richard) attempted to raise money to restore it in the 1750s but without success. The church was completely rebuilt in 1835 on the original foundations and few older features remain. The door is on the south side and is of simple construction. All the windows contain plain glass in wooden frames. Inside the church are box-pews for the rich, backless benches for the less well-off and standing room for the poor. The church contains a communion chalice dated 1547. The bell-cote contains one bell which is inscribed 'God save this church 1642'. The rope for ringing the bell dangles outside the west wall. The font is an octagonal bowl just over 1 foot high from the 14th century. The church is a delightful example of a tiny rural church; sadly it is no longer in regular use, although occasional services are still conducted. [58]

Llanfihangel Din Sylwy – ***St Michael/Sant Mihangel***

The church is situated about 1.5 miles (2.4 km) north-east of the village of Llanddona. It is necessary to cross a field to reach it.
Grid Reference SH 588 815.

This tiny church stands in a small well-maintained churchyard; it is within sight of the sea and Puffin Island (*Ynys Seiriol*) is clearly visible. The nave, chancel and chancel arch date from the 15th century, but the west wall and bell-cote are more recent. The church underwent some restoration in the 1853-4, the architect being Henry Kennedy. The door is on the south side; it has no porch. The roof of the chancel has three original trusses and the windows are 15th century. In the south wall of the chancel is a blocked doorway. Parts of the north window in the nave are formed from what is believed to be an 18th century gravestone which bears an incised design, but this is now fairly indistinct. The bell-cote houses one bell believed to date from the 14th century and bearing the inscription 'Santa Maria'. This bell was re-hung in October 2005. The church has a fine example of a carved pulpit, hexagonal in shape and ornately carved, dating from 1628. The font is an octagonal stone bowl believed to date from the 15th century. The altar is a simple wooden table. There is no stained glass, all the windows being of clear leaded glass. Inside the church are oil lamps; the church has no electricity. [59]

Llanfihangel Tre'r Beirdd – *St Michael/Sant Mihangel*
The church is situated in an area known as Maenaddwyn.
Grid Reference SH 459 837.
St Michael's church is a small, neat church within a well-maintained churchyard. The church underwent some restoration in 1811 and 1844, and was largely rebuilt in 1888 but some features of the earlier building were retained. The bell-cote houses one bell and the doorway and porch are on the north side. The north and south windows of the chancel are medieval. All the windows are of clear glass except those on the west and east walls. The east window is a fairly wide and ornate window in one light containing stained glass. In the nave are three medieval gritstone slabs with various inscribed patterns: a cross, rings, trefoils (three lobed shapes) and quatrefoils (four lobed shapes). On the north wall of the nave is a medieval stone stoup. Inside the church is a memorial (dated 1763) to Morys ap Rhisiart Morys of Pentre Eirianell, the father of the famous Morris brothers (Morrisiaid Môn). The octagonal gritstone font is of medieval origin. The church contains a 17th century plain oak chest with metal straps. In the south-west corner of the churchyard is an ancient stone cross with a circular base. Also in the churchyard (near the east wall) is a conical shaped stone set on a cylindrical base. This is about 2 feet (60 cm) tall and may have served as a boundary marker in ancient times. [60]

Llanfihangel yn Nhowyn – *St Michael/Sant Mihangel*

The church is situated 0.6 mile (1.0 km) south of the A5 road near Caergeiliog. Grid Reference SH 322 774.

The church stands in the village of Llanfihangel yn Nhowyn. A gated archway leads to the church and a small churchyard. The church was extensively rebuilt in 1862 by architects Henry Kennedy and John Rogers. It was closed by the Church in Wales a number of years ago, but more recently it has been acquired by the RAF who have an air base nearby. Most of the windows contain clear leaded glass, but there is stained glass in the east window. There is also stained glass related to the RAF in one of the windows on the south side. There is an extensive modern annexe (built in a similar style to the original church) on the west side of the building. This explains why the bell-cote is not situated at the west end. There are separate entrances for the church and annexe which is used for community purposes. [61]

Llanfihangel Ysgeifiog – *St Michael/ Sant Mihangel (New Church)*

The church is situated on the A5 on the western outskirts of the village of Gaerwen, opposite the entrance to an industrial estate.
Grid Reference SH 478 720.

This church was built in 1847 to a design by Henry Kennedy and an unknown amateur architect. It was intended to serve the growing village of Gaerwen and to replace the old church which was too far from the village (see below). Some restoration took place in 1897 under Peter S. Gregory. Entry into the churchyard is through a massively-constructed slate-roofed lychgate. At the west end the bell-cote is very elaborate and contains two bells. On the west wall there is an unusual round window of coloured glass. The north wall is supported by a number of sturdy buttresses. The east window of the chancel contains stained glass. In the north wall of the nave is a modern example of stained glass in memory of Iorwerth Thomas who was Rector of the parish from 1952 to 1981. It was a gift from his widow. Below the east window of the chancel is the grave of Richard Parry Jones who was rector of the parish for 37 years. [62]

Llanfihangel Ysgeifiog – *St Michael/ Sant Mihangel (Old Church)*

The church is situated 0.1 mile (0.2 km) off the road between Pentre Berw and Ceint. A footpath leads to the church. Access by car is not possible. Grid Reference SH 478 734.

The old church of Llanfihangel Ysgeifiog dates from the 15th century and stands in a lonely spot some distance from the village of Gaerwen. The north chapel was added in 1638 by the Holland family of Pentre Berw. There was also a south chapel but this was demolished in the 1870s. The church was abandoned when the new church was built in Gaerwen in 1847. Today it stands roofless and forlorn surrounded by a walled churchyard containing a considerable number of gravestones. The site has been cleared in recent years and is well worth a visit. The bell-cote is still in place as is the west doorway. [63]

Llanfwrog – *St Mwrog*

The church is situated 1.5 miles (2.4 km) north-west of the village of Llanfachraeth. Grid Reference SH 301 843.

A gateway with a small wooden gate leads into the churchyard. The church was rebuilt on the site of the old church in 1864, and was designed by Henry Kennedy and John Rogers. Repairs were undertaken under architect Harold Hughes in 1911. The bell-cote contains one bell which, unusually, can be rung using a handle on the outside wall. All the windows contain clear leaded glass. The east window of the chancel is of a particularly intricate design; on both sides are carved human faces. There is a vestry on the north side. The part of the churchyard immediately surrounding the church is well-maintained. The church became redundant in the 1990s, and has passed into private hands. It is in need of repairs and is currently undergoing restoration. Prior to its closure, the chancel used to contain an oak chest bearing the initials DR and HW and dated 1722. The font was a plain octagonal bowl of medieval origin. [64]

Llangadwaladr – *St Cadwaladr*

This historic church is situated near the A4080 about 0.3 mile (0.5 km) west of the village of Hermon. It is well hidden by trees.
Grid Reference SH 383 693.

It is believed that St Cadwaladr was Cadwaladr the Blessed, the last King of the British in the 7th century; it is thought he died in 664 AD. The Tudor dynasty (originally linked to Plas Penmynydd) were said to be descended from him. The church is sometimes referred to Eglwys Ail (*The Wattle Church*) suggesting that it was not originally built of stone. An impressive lychgate, clearly of some antiquity, leads to the churchyard. The bell-cote is topped by a weather-vane; it houses two bells but has room for three. The earliest part of the present church (Figure 10), which is now a Grade I listed building, is the nave which dates from the 12th or 13th century. There is a blocked doorway which dates from this period in the south wall of the nave. In the 14th century the church was extended by the addition of the present chancel. The church has close links with the Welsh court at Aberffraw and in the north wall of the chancel is an inscribed stone commemorating King Cadfan of Gwynedd (who died about 625 AD), who was Cadwaladr's grandfather. The stone bears the Latin inscription 'Catamanus rex sapientisimus, opinatisimus omnium regum' ('Cadfan, the wisest and most renowned of all kings'). The history of the church is linked to two prominent land-owning Anglesey families, the Owen family of Bodowen and the Meyricks of Bodorgan Hall. The stained glass east window of the chancel was a gift from Meuric ap Llywelyn and his wife in thanks for the safe return of their son Owain from the Battle of Bosworth in 1485. It is one of the finest examples of stained glass windows in Anglesey. The stained glass is in three lights: the centre light shows an image of the crucifixion with Saints John and Mary on either side and lower down an image of King Cadwaladr; the left and right hand lights show members of the Meyrick family. The stained glass was reset in a modern window during a restoration in 1857-59 that required the addition of new stained glass because the new window was larger. Richard Meyrick was responsible for the addition of the north chapel in 1640; it was rebuilt in 1801 and

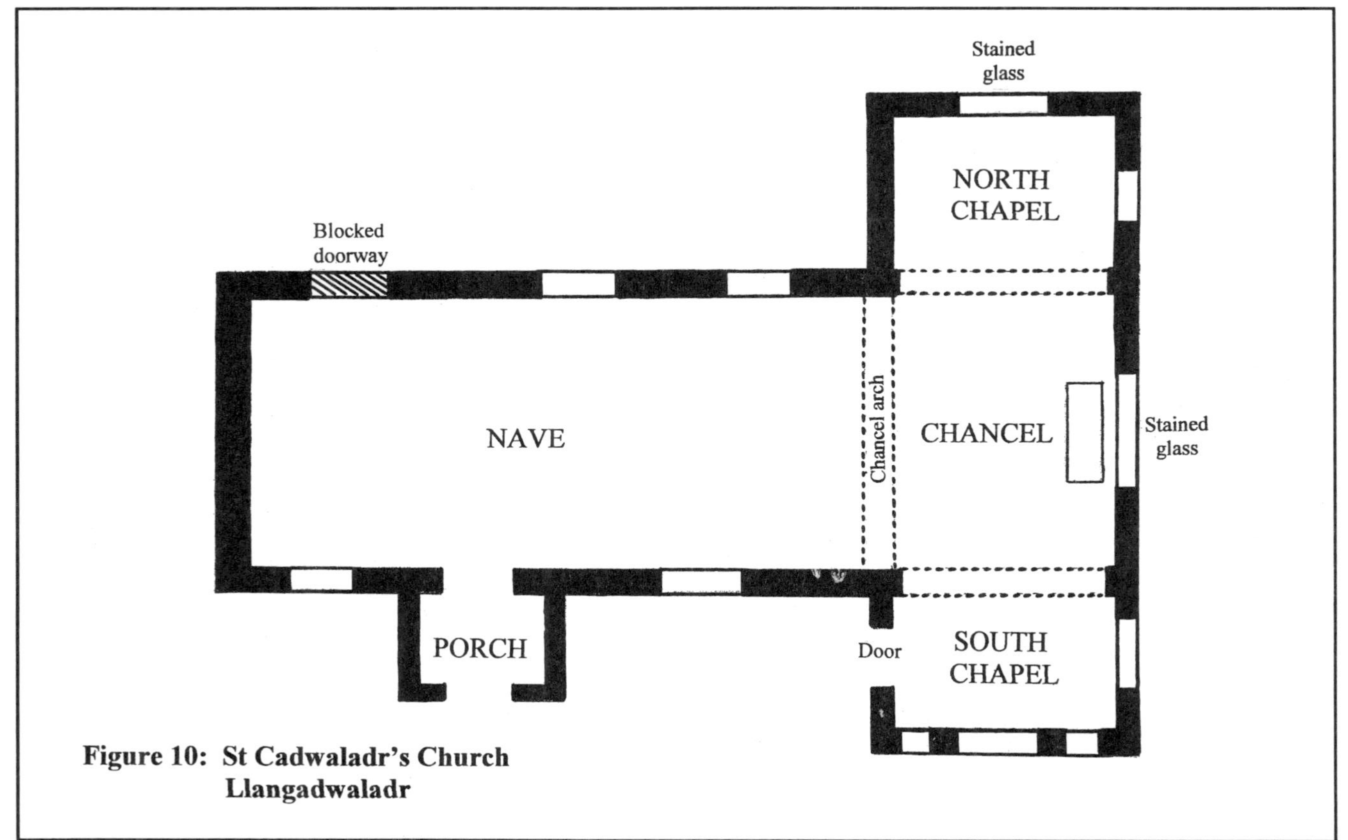

Figure 10: St Cadwaladr's Church Llangadwaladr

further restored in 1907. In 1661 Colonel Hugh Owen of Bodowen financed a south chapel built in a Gothic style. Originally the south chapel contained stained glass in the south and east windows and a painted ceiling; both of these features have long since disappeared. The chapels contain memorials to members of the families who built them. The church is undergoing a major restoration in 2005-6, including reslating the roof, conservation work on the stained glass in the east window of the chancel and repairing the iron gate. The work is supported by the Heritage Lottery fund as well as other sources of funding. In the north side of the churchyard is a huge carved Celtic cross commemorating members of the Meyrick family. St Cadwaladr's church is one of the most historic churches in Anglesey and is worth a close examination. [65]

Llangadwaladr – *St Meirian, Llanfeirian*

The church was located near the entrance to Parc Bach farm, near Hermon. Grid Reference SH 388 686.

It is thought that St Meirian's Church (also known as Merthyr Meirian) was in use until about 1750. It was a chapel of ease used by families from nearby mansion houses such as Bodorgan Hall. Inside the church the pews were said to have been lined with green baize. Historical accounts suggest that the church was quite small, about 7m by 17m. The site where the church stood is still clearly visible; it is a roughly circular walled enclosure which is now wooded and overgrown with no obvious trace remaining.

Llangaffo – *St Caffo*

The church stands near the centre of this small village.
Grid Reference SH 446 685.

It is believed that there may have been a monastery on or near this site at one time. It was known as Merthyr Caffo. The present church stands in a slight hollow and was designed by John Weightman and Matthew Hadfield of Sheffield and built in 1847 very near to the location of the old church. Access to the churchyard is through a simple lychgate. This lychgate incorporates the 15th century doorway from the old church. On the site are a number of carved and inscribed stones believed to date from the 7th to the 13th centuries. Some are to be found within the church, in the churchyard wall and six others stand outside the north door. On the west side stands the impressive church tower and steeple; this is a landmark visible for many miles. Part of the tower and the south wall of the church are covered in render making them less attractive than the north wall. The nave and chancel have stained glass windows. The font is a 12th century circular tub-shaped bowl on a modern plinth. At the highest point of the well-maintained churchyard, on the north side, stands a Celtic cross which commemorates those who died in two World Wars. Also in the churchyard is the grave of entrepreneur Hugh Hughes who owned coalmines at Pentre Berw and Glantraeth. He died in 1876. [66]

Llangefni – *St Cyngar*

The church is situated about 0.2 mile (0.3 km) from the town centre, just off Church Street. Grid Reference SH 458 759.

St Cyngar (a descendent of Cunedda Wledig) established his church on the banks of the river Cefni and near to St Cyngar's well (situated about 100 metres from the church on the Nant y Pandy path and restored in 2000). The area has been known occasionally as Llangyngar in the past, but the name Llangefni is now long established. The present church was built in 1824 after the old church was demolished. The exterior stonework is of a conglomerate stone and sandstone. The chancel appears fairly short in relation to the length of the nave. The door is on the west side of the tower. In the porch can be found a 5th century inscribed gravestone (the Culidorus Stone), a cylindrical bowl font about 18 inches high with a crudely-patterned rim, believed to be from the 12th century as well as a sundial (dated 1673) and a chest dated 1811. In the tower are three bronze bells dating from 1868 and a clock presented to the church by James Warren Bulkeley of Beaumaris in 1822. Inside the church is an octagonal font, and a Bishop's chair which was presented to the church in 1835. This chair is used by the bishop when he visits the church. There is seating for 200 worshippers. In the east window of the chancel there is stained glass which portrays Jesus as the Good Shepherd, as well as images of Saint James and Saint John. In the south walls of the nave and chancel are two other windows which contain stained glass. The church underwent some restoration in 1858 when a vestry was added and repairs made to the roof and walls; the stoutly-constructed lychgate was added in 1890. The chancel was added in 1889. Further repairs took place in 1954. In the churchyard most of the gravestones have been laid flat for ease of maintenance. In the churchyard there is a bronze sundial bearing the date 1673. [67]

Llangefni – *St Joseph's Roman Catholic Church/ Eglwys Babyddol St Joseff*

The church is situated in Penmynydd Road 0.5 mile (0.8 km) from the town centre. Grid Reference SH 466 756.

Roman Catholics have worshipped in Llangefni since 1941. The present building was consecrated in May 1971; it replaced a smaller church in Bridge Street. It is a fairly large red brick building with a tiled roof. On the roof is mounted a large metal cross. Above the doorway windows are arranged in the shape of a cross. [68]

Llangeinwen – *St Ceinwen*

The church is situated on a sharp bend on the A4080 road just outside Dwyran. Grid Reference SH 440 658.

The cell was founded by St Ceinwen (see also Cerrigceinwen) about 590 AD. The parish of Llangeinwen has also been known as Clynnog Fach because the parish lands once belonged to the wealthy church of St Beuno at Clynnog Fawr (on the Llŷn Peninsula) in medieval times. The earliest parts of the present building, the north and south walls of the nave, are from the 12th century. Some restoration took place in 1812, financed by Lord Boston. In 1829 (not 1839 as some sources state) the tower and the north chapel were built and several windows were added. Further restoration was carried out in 1841 and in 1928 by Harold Hughes and William G. Williams. Incised gravestones, believed to be about 1000 years old, have been set into the north-west buttress of the nave. The porch, on the south side, contains a record of those parishioners who perished in the First World War; it contains no fewer than 80 names. The leaded windows are of plain glass. Inside the church a strange arched shape of stones can be seen on the north wall of the nave; the same feature is also visible from the outside. This is a blocked 12th century doorway. In the chancel, the roof timbers are hidden by a ceiling. The font is a decorated circular bowl on a square base and is believed to be 13th century. The church also contains some early 19th century brass chandeliers. The exterior walls of the church are covered in an unusual render which has in places been repaired. The tower walls are encrusted with yellow lichen. St Ceinwen's church is a attractive rural church of fairly unusual design; it is well-maintained and the churchyard is particularly tidy with colourful flower-boxes placed on the south side of the church. [69]

Llangoed – *St Cawrdaf*

The church of St Cawdraf stands about a mile from the village of Llangoed up a steep hill. Grid Reference SH 611 805.

St Cawrdaf is believed to have been a disciple of St Seiriol. This cruciform church was virtually rebuilt in 1881 under the direction of Henry Kennedy. The north transept, however, dates from 1612 (this date can be seen on a stone set above its north window). A small vestry was added on the north side in 1910. On the west side is a simple bell-cote which houses one bell. On the west wall is a stone bearing the dates 1881 and 1613. In the porch is a small plain 15th century stoup. The chancel and north transept have stained glass windows. Inside the church there is a 17th century pulpit bearing the inscription 'E.I. 1622'. The font is a 14th century plain octagonal bowl and beneath a trapdoor is a baptismal pool. A 12th century gravestone with an incised cross forms the step to the east door of the north transept. There is an elaborate candelabrum, dated 1818, in the centre of the church. [70]

Llangristiolus – *St Cristiolus*

The church is situated near the A5 south of Llangefni.
Grid Reference SH 450 736.

The church of St Cristiolus is situated on elevated ground above the Malltraeth marsh near the A5. The church stands in close proximity to a small cottage, and access to the churchyard is through a simple lychgate. It is believed that St Cristiolus founded his cell here in 610 AD. The present church dates from the 12th and 13th centuries. It was restored in 1851 by Henry Kennedy when the north and south walls of the chancel were rebuilt, but the 13th century chancel arch was retained. The east window of the chancel and the eastern window in the north wall of the chancel are 16th century. The other windows are modern. The church has an ornate bell-cote containing one bell. Most of the windows are of plain leaded glass, but the east window of the chancel contains coloured glass. The only stained glass is found in the north wall of the nave. This impressive modern window is in memory of Hugh and Eira Jones of Tŷ Newydd, Llangristiolus who died in the early 1990s. The interior of the church tends to feel long and narrow, but is in a good state of repair. Some steps lead to the octagonal pulpit. The font is a 12th century circular gritstone bowl having six decorated panels. The reredos behind the altar is of plain wood. On the north wall of the nave is a memorial to those who died in the First World War. A memorial stone to those who died in the Second World War is outside the church. The churchyard is on two levels, the most recent burials being on the north side. In the churchyard near to the east wall of the chancel is the grave of the Reverend Richard Owen (1839-1887). He was one of Wales' most famous Calvinistic Methodist preachers in his day, although he is little remembered now. [71]

Llangwyfan – *St Mary/Santes Fair (New Church)*

The church is situated about 1.5 miles (2.4 km) north-west of Aberffraw on a minor road leading off the A4080. Grid Reference SH 344 710.

This Victorian church (now in the parish of Llanfaelog and Llangwyfan) dates from 1871 and was a replacement for the old church (see below). The architects were Henry Kennedy and

Gustavus Hamilton O'Donoghue. The church authorities were clearly taking no chances that the new church should suffer the same fate as the old one (see below) as it was built a mile from the coast. It stands in a quiet rural location. A simple gateway leads into the churchyard and the porch is on the north side. The bell-cote houses one bell. Most of the windows are of clear leaded glass, but the east window of the chancel contains stained glass. The altar is a simple wooden table separated from the rest of the church by a simple altar rail. Near the door stands a font with an ornate wooden cover. On the north and south walls of the chancel are painted the phrases 'Fy ngwaed i sydd ddiod yn awr' (*My blood is a drink now*) and 'Fy nghnawd sydd fwyd yn wir' (*My flesh is food indeed*). [72]

Llangwyfan – *St Cwyfan (Old Church)*

The church is situated on a small island 1.3 miles (2.1 km) south-west of Aberffraw. A minor road leads to a bay known as Porth Cwyfan, from where the church can be accessed by foot at low tide.

Grid Reference SH 336 683.

St Cwyfan is believed to have been Irish and a possibly disciple of St Beuno; it is thought that he established his church here in the 7th century. The present church building is originally from the 12th century and it stood on the mainland overlooking the sea. Reconstruction took place in the 14th century and much of the walls are from this period. A north aisle and an arcade were added in the 16th century. The church was still on the mainland early in the 17th century but subsequently, rapid erosion created an island. It is believed the island was formed about the end of the 17th century. Erosion must have been very severe because the church's second aisle was demolished (in the early 19th century) as the sea eroded the island. The arches of the arcade were filled with masonry and this can be seen clearly in the north wall inside the church. On both sides of the south doorway is a red sandstone block, both originally carved but now too weathered to be decipherable. The doorway had a porch at one time. The remains of a causeway linking the island to the mainland can be seen when the tide is low. When tides prevented worshippers from reaching the island, services were held at Plas Llangwyfan (1 mile away) in a specially consecrated area. By 1871 the church had been replaced by a new church (St Mary's), and by the end of the 19th century the island church was in a state of neglect and was roofless. It was restored in 1893 by Harold Hughes, the well-known architect and archaeologist from Llanfairfechan. A sum of £82 was raised to repair and reslate the roof. Erosion of what remained of the island was halted by building a strong stone wall to enclose it. Inside the church the great antiquity of the roof beams is apparent. The internal walls are whitewashed and the floor is concrete. There is a simple wooden altar and pulpit. There are chairs for the congregation. The bell-cote has no bell; however, there is a bell on a wooden frame inside the church. The windows are plainly of considerable antiquity (probably 14th or 15th century) but there is no stained glass. There are several gravestones in the churchyard, the oldest bearing the date 1650 although the others are from the 18th and 19th centuries. Many graves were washed away by the sea as the churchyard was eroded. The church is now in the combined parish of Llanfaelog and Llangwyfan. A restoration project is planned for 2006. Services are still conducted here a few times a year, typically between June and August. [73]

Llangwyllog – *St Cwyllog*

The church is situated 3.0 miles (4.8 km) north-west of Llangefni, just off the B5111. Grid Reference SH 434 796.

St Cwyllog's church stands in a hollow in a quiet rural location. It has a sloping churchyard. North of the church is a stream and the Amlwch railway branch line, now disused. The church was built with a continuous nave and chancel probably in the 15th century or possibly earlier. An annexe (with its own door) was subsequently added, probably in the 16th century, at the western end. The annexe contains an 18th century fireplace. The bell-cote contains one bell dated 1662. The doorway on the north side is from the 15th century. The east window of the chancel, which is in three lights, is from the 15th century and contains stained glass. The windows of the western annexe are not all of the same style. There is a combined pulpit and reading desk bearing the date

1769. The pews are from the 18th century. The font is a cylindrical bowl from the 13th century; it is unusual because the carving work on it was left incomplete. The church underwent restoration in 1812 funded by the 7th Viscount Bulkeley. Further restoration work took place in 1854 under the direction of architect D. Roberts of Beaumaris. [74]

Llanidan – *St Nidan (New Church)*
The church stands on the A4080 on the northern outskirts of the village of Brynsiencyn. Grid Reference SH 489 674.
The new church of St Nidan dates from 1841. It is of fairly unusual appearance, not at all typical of Anglesey churches in its stonework or the shape of the castellated tower which houses a clock which faces west and east. The porch under the clock tower provides access to a balcony. The organ and the vestry are in unusually-shaped rooms off the transepts. The cylindrical font on an octagonal base is believed to be from the 13th century and therefore from the old church (see below). There are two bells from the old church, one is from the 14th century and bears the inscription E:D:A:N, and the other bears the name Thomas ap Meredith and is from the 15th century. The chancel was added in 1882. The ornate stained glass in the north transept was donated to the church in memory of Anna Maria Evans (1898-1929). In the churchyard next to the north wall of the church is the grave of Sir Ellis Jones Ellis-Griffiths (1860-1926) who was raised in Brynsiencyn and was Liberal MP for Anglesey from 1893 to 1918. He favoured the disestablishment of the Welsh Anglican Church and was one of those responsible for steering the Act through the House of Commons. [75]

Llanidan – *St Nidan (Old Church)*
The remains of the old parish church of Llanidan lies on a lane leading from the village of Brynsiencyn towards the Menai Straits.
rid Reference SH 495 669.
St Nidan first established his cell in the 7th century. The ruined church, which stands only a quarter of a mile from the Straits, dates from about the 15th century. It was a double-aisled church

with a south chapel and a south porch. The church contained some interesting antiquities, window tracery (ornamental stonework around windows) and a reliquary said to contain the remains of a saint. The stoup in the south porch reputedly never dries up and traditionally its waters were said to have healing properties. The church was almost entirely demolished in 1844, but the 15th century arcade and the western end were retained. Some bells from the 14th and 15th century were moved to the new church as was the 13th century font. The remains of the church were used as a mortuary chapel for a time. Some restoration work has taken place and it is still used as a private chapel for nearby Plas Llanidan. The remains can be seen through a locked gateway and gravestones are still visible in the cemetery. Thomas Williams (1737-1802) who made his fortune from the copper mines of Mynydd Parys was buried in the churchyard. However, 30 years later his remains were reburied in Llandegfan churchyard. [76]

Llaniestyn – *St Iestyn*

This church is located about 0.6 mile (1.0 km) east of the village of Llanddona. Grid Reference SH 585 796.

A religious cell is believed to have been founded here in the 7th century by St Iestyn, thought to be a nephew of St Cybi. The nave and chancel (which are undivided) of the present building were once believed to be 14th century. However, during the 20th century, a narrow 12th century door was discovered in the west wall of the nave; this suggests that at least part of the church is of this period and therefore older than had been supposed. The south chapel was a later addition to the nave and chancel. The south door is within an unusually wide porch having a carved wooden fascia. The doorway itself is believed to be from the 15th century. The east window of the chancel is particularly old and is believed to be from the 15th century. There is no stained glass in any of the windows. The west wall has the original bell-cote containing one bell. Inside the church the walls are whitewashed. The font is a cylindrical bowl with a carved surface and is probably from the 12th century. The opening to the 15th century south chapel is spanned by a huge wooden beam. On the west wall of this chapel is an image of St Iestyn carved on a grey stone slab. It shows a bearded man dressed as a hermit with a cloak and hood. The slab is believed to be 14th century. It bears a Latin inscription which translates as 'Here lies Iestyn to whom Gwenllian ferch Madog and Gruffydd ap Gwilym offered this image for the health of their souls'. The church was restored under the direction of Beaumaris architect D. Roberts in 1865. The church underwent some further restoration in the 1950s. [77]

Llanllibio – *St Llibio*

Grid Reference SH 331 817.

The church of Llanllibio was about 0.8 mile (1.3 km) north of Bodedern. It was a chapel of ease to Llantrisant. It was closed in the 17th century and a south chapel was added to Llantrisant church (the old church) to accommodate worshippers from Llanllibio. In 1776 St Llibio's church was described as being in ruins and only tiny traces of it can now be seen. A single slate memorial marks the spot where the church stood.

Llannerch-y-Medd – *St Mary/Santes Fair*

The church is situated in the centre of the village.

Grid Reference SH 418 841.

The fairly large church is approached through a particularly large and unusual lychgate which contains a small bell-cote (with one bell) and a clock. A stone inserted into the lychgate bears the date 1755. Unfortunately the lychgate appears to have suffered at the hands of vandals and has been daubed in graffiti. The original church on this site dated from medieval times but was almost completely rebuilt in the 1840s and only two older features remain – the lower part of the tower and a doorway from the nave to the tower. The church was further restored by Henry Kennedy in 1856. The large tower is unusual in that it appears to contain a belfry (the louvred panels being apparent) but also a large bell-cote housing one bell. The porch is on the north side; it leads to the massive church door. The font is an octagonal bowl probably from the 14th century. The church suffered storm damage in the late 1990s and although the roof has been repaired, further restoration has been delayed; all the windows of the church are boarded up and the building is not in use at present. Services are conducted in a nearby chapel. [78]

Llanrhuddlad – *St Rhuddlad*

The church stands 1.5 miles (2.4 km) west of the village of Llanrhuddlad near Church Bay (Porth Swtan). Grid Reference SH 306 896.

The religious cell is believed to have been established about 570 AD by Saint Rhuddlad, the daughter of the King of Leinster (one of the ancient provinces of Ireland). The lychgate leads into a large neat churchyard with comparatively few gravestones but inhabited by a number of rabbits. To the west can be seen superb views of the sea and Holyhead Mountain. The present church was designed by Henry Kennedy and completed in 1858 near the site of the previous church. When this church was being demolished in 1857, a 9th or 10th century bronze handbell was found in the church wall. The tower and stone spire of the church are very prominent local landmarks and have led to the nearby popular beach being called Church Bay, although Porth Swtan is its correct name. All the windows contain plain leaded glass except the east window of the chancel which contains stained glass. The font is a plain medieval cylindrical bowl. In the chancel are two upholstered chairs from the 17th century. The Reverend Morris Williams (better known by his bardic name Nicander) was rector here (as well as at nearby Llanfflewin) from 1859 to 1874. He was a well-known poet and hymn-writer. [79]

Llanrhwydrus – *St Rhwydrus*

The church is situated in an isolated spot (near a farm called Tyn Llan) not far from Cemlyn Bay 3 miles (5 km) west of Cemaes.
Grid Reference SH 322 932.

To the west of Cemlyn Bay near some marshland lies the pretty little church of Llanrhwydrus which is one of the oldest religious sites in Anglesey. It was founded about 570 AD by Saint Rhwydrus, son of Rhodrin the King of Connaught (an ancient province of Ireland). The nave of the present church dates from the 12th century and the chancel and chancel arch are from the 13th century. It is not clear when the north chapel was built. The tiny south doorway is probably 12th century. The church bell bears an inscription and is dated 1721. The east window of the chancel is 15th century. At the west end there is a gallery which has a beam dated 1776. The font is a plain cylindrical bowl from the 12th century. The church has no electricity. Services are still conducted here occasionally. Llanrhwydrus church is a most attractive little church and is well worth seeing. [80]

Llansadwrn – *St Sadwrn*

The church stands at the roadside 0.8 mile (0.8 km) south-west of the village of Llansadwrn. Grid Reference SH 554 758.

The fairly modern lychgate contains a re-used beam dated 1735 and has a roof made of massive pieces of slate. The church was originally established in 520 AD and underwent repairs in 1829 and 1839. It was rebuilt in 1881 by architect Henry Kennedy on the foundations of the previous church and the north porch was added at about the same time. It has a continuous nave and chancel. The date of the north chapel is unclear. On the west end is an impressive bell-cote containing two bells. Inside the church is a stone, probably from the sixth century, which records the burial of Saturninus and his wife. This stone was discovered nearby in 1742. It is believed that Saturninus is not the same person as St Sadwrn to whom the church is dedicated. On the gable of the north chapel are two 15th century corbels. One depicts a human head, the other is that of a bear. In 1895 further restoration occurred when the chancel was re-roofed and refurbished. The church has a number of stained-glass windows. The font is an octagonal bowl made of Penmon marble and dates from 1737. In the churchyard can be seen the grave of Sir Andrew Crombie Ramsey (1814-1891), a pioneer of north Wales geology and the son-in-law of the Reverend James Williams and his wife Frances (see *Llanfairynghornwy*). His headstone is a massive glacial boulder. On either side of this grave are the graves of two former rectors of the parish, David Lewis (died 1948) and Evan Evans (died 1915). On a grassy area in front of the church stands a massive (almost 4 metres tall) beautifully carved Celtic cross, a memorial to Hugh

Stewart McCorquodale of nearby Gadlys who died while serving in the armed forces in South Africa in 1900. Not far from the church are a burial chamber and standing stones (SH 567 775). [81]

Llantrisant – ***St Afran (or Gafran), St Ieuan & St Sannan (Old Church)***

The church is situated in an isolated spot south-east of Llanddeusant. Grid Reference SH 349 841.

The old church of Llantrisant (now a Grade 2* listed building) became redundant in 1899 when the new parish church was built. It is set in a secluded and peaceful location. The continuous nave and chancel date from the late 14th century. The south doorway is from the 15th century. In the 17th century a south chapel was added for worshippers from nearby Llanllibio after their church had closed. The bell-cote is from the 17th century. The roof of the nave and chancel have a ceiling; the roof of the chapel is original. It has a 19th century combined pulpit and reading desk. In the nave is an oak chest dating from 1684. The font is from the 12th century. There are a number of memorials inside the church, some dating to the 17th century. St Afran's Holy Well is near the lychgate. Llantrisant once had four chapels of ease: Llechcynfarwy, Gwredog, Llanllibio and Rhodogeidio. This was the first church in Anglesey to be acquired by the Friends of Friendless Churches Society. [82]

Llantrisant – ***St Afran (or Gafran), St Ieuan & St Sannan (New Church)***

The church is on a minor road about three miles north-east of Bodedern. Grid Reference SH 364 836.

This church stands on a quiet country lane. A small gate leads into a fairly large well-maintained churchyard with comparatively few burials on the north side. The church was designed by Peter S. Gregory and the foundation stone laid by Lady Meyrick in 1898. The church was completed in 1899 and was intended to replace the old church (about a mile to the north-west). The porch is on the south side. The roof slates are of an unusual light colour with red ridge tiles. The bell-cote contains one bell. There is stained glass in the east window of the chancel and in the south walls of the nave. Elsewhere the windows contain coloured leaded glass. [83]

Llanwenllwyfo – *St Gwenllwyfo (New church)*
The church is situated 0.5 miles (0.8 km) north of Dulas Beach.
Grid Reference SH 477 893.
The old church of Llanwenllwyfo (dedicated to the female saint St Gwenllwyfo) was in a poor state of repair and was too small for the congregation in the 1840s. When the idea of building a new church was first suggested, the inhabitants of Nebo (the most populated part to the north of the parish) were keen to have the church in their neighbourhood. The church of Llanwenllwyfo had always had a close association with the nearby Llys Dulas estate who opposed any plan to site the new church at Nebo. It was therefore built in a fairly isolated and very tranquil spot near to the Llys Dulas estate and not far from Dulas Bay. The foundation stone was laid in 1854 by Gwen Gertrude Hughes, who was nine years old and heiress of Llys Dulas. The church was designed by Henry Kennedy and was completed in 1856. The total cost was £1,417, of which £936 was donated by Gertrude Lady Dinorben (Gwen's mother). She was the widow of Lord Dinorben (William Lewis Hughes), at one time an MP. The church stands on a large sloping site and is impressively large; it has a steeply-pitched slate roof which gives the interior a sense of space. Inside the church there is an interesting octagonal font and a 17th century brass plate (on the west wall of the nave) from the old church commemorating Marcelie Lloyd and the family of nearby Llys Dulas. On the west wall of the nave there can also be found a slate tablet listing those who contributed to the building costs of the church. The octagonal wooden pulpit is in the same style as the choir stalls. The church is noteworthy because it contains considerable amounts of impressive 15th and 16th century Flemish stained glass in the windows of the nave and chancel. These came from the collection of Sir Thomas Arundell Neave (Gwen Gertrude Hughes married into the Neave family) and were presented to the church in 1876. Some of the stained glass came from a monastery in Louvain in Belgium. The east window of the

chancel is particularly impressive and contains images which include the crucifixion, the Holy Trinity and the Wise Men visiting the baby Jesus. On the walls of the chancel are tablets in memory of Gwen Gertrude Hughes (who is buried in a vault below the church), her mother, her husband Sir Arundell Neave and her son. Also in the chancel is a glass case which houses a beautifully-crafted model of the church made from matches by William Parry of Amlwch. In 2002 the church underwent extensive restoration including the reslating of the roof and the cleaning of the stained glass. This church contains a wealth of interesting items which are worth seeing. [84]

Llanwenllwyfo – *St Gwenllwyfo (Old Parish Church)*
The church was located near the mansion of Llys Dulas.
Grid Reference SH 488 902.
The old church of St Gwenllwyfo was a small medieval building with a continuous nave and chancel. It is said to have been restored about 1610 and again in the 18th and 19th centuries. By the mid-19th century it was considered too small to serve the parish, and a new church was built. Consequently, the old church of Llanwenllwyfo was abandoned in 1856 and is now a roofless ruin. The bell from the old church (probably 18th century) is now kept at the new church. The ruins as well as the old cemetery stand near the manorhouse of Llys Dulas, well hidden by trees. [85]

Llanynghenedl – *St Enghenedl*
The church site stands in the village of Llanynghenedl, near the A5025.
Grid Reference SH 317 810.
The church of St Enghenedl had a continuous nave and chancel together with a north vestry and south porch. It was rebuilt in the 19th century, but declined in importance when a church was built at the growing nearby village of Valley, also in the parish of Llanynghenedl. The church contained a font which was a plain circular bowl from the 12th century. The church was demolished in the 1980s; the lychgate still remains as does the churchyard and its gravestones. Unfortunately the site is now very overgrown. [86]

Llanynghenedl – *St Michael/Sant Mihangel, Valley*
This church is situated on the A5 road in the village of Valley.
Grid Reference SH 293 794.
This church was built in 1867 in a 15th century Gothic style. It was intended to serve the expanding community of Valley in the south of the parish of Llanynghenedl. The neat-looking church stands in a small well-maintained churchyard containing a number of burials. It is a cruciform church with a slated roof and red ridge tiles. The bell-cote contains one bell. The north and south windows of the transepts contain an unusual patterned coloured glass; there is stained glass in the east and south windows of the chancel and the east window of the south transept. On the north side there is an extension to the building which has a separate doorway. [87]

Llechcynfarwy – *St Cynfarwy*
This church is situated on the B5112 about 3 miles north of the A5.
Grid Reference SH 381 811.
Llechcynfarwy church was once a chapel of ease to Llantrisant. The church was almost completely rebuilt to a design by Henry Kennedy and Gustavus Hamilton O'Donoghue in 1868 when the north porch was added. It is undivided into nave and chancel. The south chapel dates from the 17th century; a stone in its south wall bears the date and initials 1664 WB. The bell-cote contains one bell. The only stained glass is in the east window; the other windows contain clear leaded panes. It has a 12th century decorated circular font (just over 1 foot high). Inside the church is an ornate memorial to Helen Bold of nearby Tre'r Ddôl (dated 1631) and another to Margaret Williams of Erianell (1764). Long-cist graves (where bodies were buried within a coffin made of flat stones) were discovered near the church in 1926. [88]

Llechylched Old Church – *St Ylched*
This church stood about 0.9 mile (1.5 km) south-west of Bryngwran.
Grid Reference SH 340 767.
This church closed in 1841 when the new church (in the village of Bryngwran) was built. The churchyard wall can still be seen; within the enclosure a large cross and some graves are still visible but the church itself has totally disappeared.

Llechylched with Ceirchiog – *Holy Trinity/Y Drindod Sanctaidd*
The church stands in the village of Bryngwran, within yards of the A5. Grid Reference SH 351 774.
Holy Trinity was a new church built in 1841 and its style is different to most Anglesey churches. The architects were John Lloyd and William Williams. Some restoration was undertaken in 1958. It is of a rather chunky 17th century Jacobean style. It replaced a previous parish church on a different site (see above). It is divided into a nave and chancel but the latter is unusually small. The windows of the nave contain coloured leaded panes, but the chancel window contains patterned stained glass. The large bell-cote (having one bell) is above the porch at the opposite end to the chancel. The church does not have the usual east-west alignment of most churches. The parishes of Llechylched and Ceirchiog were amalgamated for ecclesiastical purposes in 1842. [89]

Malltraeth – *Church of Christ the King/ Eglwys Crist y Brenin*
(see Trefdraeth)

Menai Bridge – *St Mary/Santes Fair* (see Llandysilio)

Menai Bridge – *St Tysilio* (see Llandysilio)

Menai Bridge – *St Anne's Roman Catholic Church/ Eglwys Babyddol Santes Anne*
This church is in Dale Street, Menai Bridge. Grid Reference SH 555 721.
This church was built in 1956 and is a small church of modern construction on a site slightly higher than the road. Much more recently a church hall was also added to the site. A path from the flat-roofed lychgate leads to the church which is obscured by trees. [90]

Newborough – *St Peter/Sant Pedr*
The church is situated 0.3 mile (0.5 km) south-west of the village square on a minor road leading to Llanddwyn beach.
Grid Reference SH 420 655.
Newborough was created by Edward I for the inhabitants of

Llanfaes when they were moved to make way for his plans for Beaumaris. The area was previously known as Rhosyr (which may be a contraction of Rhos Fair – Mary's Moor), and had been the site of a Welsh royal court with a church dedicated to St Ano and later St Mary. Now dedicated to St Peter, the church has the distinction of being the longest in Anglesey. The bell-cote at the west end contains two bells. The chancel and the eastern part of the nave are probably 14th century. The nave was extended during the 16th century. The nave once had a north doorway, but this is now blocked. The south porch is early 16th century. The present church was restored in 1850 by Henry Kennedy and again by him in 1886 when the vestry and the chancel arch were added. The east window of the chancel (which contains stained glass) is from the 14th century. The cylindrical font is decorated with three carved panels and a fourth panel is blank; it dates from the 12th century. There are some interesting 14th century gravestones in the walls of the chancel. One of these shows an image of a priest holding a chalice while his head rests on a cushion. In the churchyard near to the south wall of the church is a memorial to those who died in both World Wars. In the churchyard can be seen the impressive grave of Sir John Prichard-Jones who died in 1917. He endowed the village of Newborough with the Pritchard-Jones Institute in 1905. [91]

Newborough – *St Thomas Mission Church/ Eglwys Genhadol Sant Thomas*

This church is situated at the junction of the A4080 and the B4421.
Grid Reference SH 423 657.

The Mission Church of St Thomas (known locally as Eglwys Bach) was built in the latter half of the 19th century. One wonders why a mission church was built here since the parish church of St Peter stands only half a mile away. St Thomas' Church is a simple building with plain frosted glass windows. It has a simple bell-cote at the west end, and the porch is on the north side. There are no burials in the area around the church. The church is no longer in use, but is now being developed by a community group for the use of the villagers. [92]

Newborough – *St Dwynwen, Llanddwyn*

A minor road branches off the A4080 in Newborough square and through a forest towards a car park at Llanddwyn Beach. A parking fee is charged. The church stands 0.8 mile (1.3 km) from car the car park. Grid Reference SH 386 627.

St Dwynwen was the daughter of King Brychan of Brycheiniog. She became the patron saint of Welsh lovers. St Dwynwen's day is celebrated on 25 January. According to legend she established this church in the 5th/6th century after a broken love affair with a man called Maelon Dafodrill. When a church was erected on the site it became one of richest in Anglesey in the 15th and 16th century, and the site was once a place of pilgrimage. The remains of the cruciform church of St Dwynwen stands on the delightful island (or more accurately, the isthmus) of Llanddwyn. It was extensively rebuilt in the 15th century but now little more than the 16th century chancel remains, surrounded by a circular churchyard. The south window of the chancel is still intact; the east and north windows partly remain. The north and south transepts were also from the 16th century but only a few traces of them now remain. The nearby Latin cross (erected 1897) commemorates Saint Dwynwen; the modern Celtic cross commemorates all those who are buried on the island. Sir Clough Williams-Ellis, the architect and designer of Port Meirion, planned to rebuild St Dwynwen's church in the early 20th century but the First World War prevented this from being carried out. Some say that St Dwynwen's holy well can be found nearby. However, others believe that it actually lies some distance to the north and is not on Llanddwyn island at all. Although reaching the church involves walking some distance, the church and Llanddwyn island are well worth visiting. [93]

Penmon – *St Seiriol*

The church is situated on a minor road about 4 miles (6.4 km) north-east of Beaumaris. Grid Reference SH 630 807.

This site is one of the earliest and most important holy sites in Anglesey; it has a small cluster of buildings. The religious settlement may have been founded here by Cynlas who may have been a brother or cousin of St Seiriol who took over in the 6th century. In 971 AD the Vikings destroyed the wooden buildings of the church, and following this a stone church was built. This church was rebuilt in the 12th century, probably between 1120 and 1170. Later in the same century the tower and the transepts were added. By the beginning of the 15th century the site had become an Augustinian Priory. Rebuilding took place again in the 15th century and in 1855 when the chancel, north transept and the east wall of the south transept were rebuilt to designs by architects John Weightman, Edward Goldie and Matthew Hadfield of Sheffield. The church is noteworthy from an architectural standpoint, the nave and transepts being very fine examples of Norman architecture (Figure 11). The tower has a squat pyramidal spire. The church houses a 12th century stone carving of the fertility figure *Sheila-na-gig* on the west wall of the south transept. Such figures are usually associated with Norman churches. Also in the south transept is a 10th century Celtic cross; one of the arms of the cross was cut off because it was used as a lintel in one of the site's monastic buildings. The south transept also houses arcading from the 12th century. The window of the south transept contains some fragments of 15th stained glass originally from the east window of the chancel. A 13th century bronze plaque of Limoges enamel discovered near the altar during the 1855 restoration is mounted in a small glass case on the north wall of the chancel. The nave of the church contains a cross dating from about 1000 AD. Formerly in a nearby deer park, it was taken to the church for safekeeping in 1977. The nave also contains a 10th century font; originally this was probably the base of the cross in the south transept and was modified for use as a font in the 19th century. Previously a 12th century pillar piscina (also in the nave) was used as a font. The impressive tower arch can be clearly seen in the east end of the nave. There is little natural light in the nave – both its windows are small and high up. Outside, above the 12th century south door of the nave is the carved figure of a dragon. The chancel is the only part of the church now used for services. It contains a number of stained glass windows, all of which are modern. The whole church was refurbished in 2005 with new lighting in the nave and south transept. The church is well worth

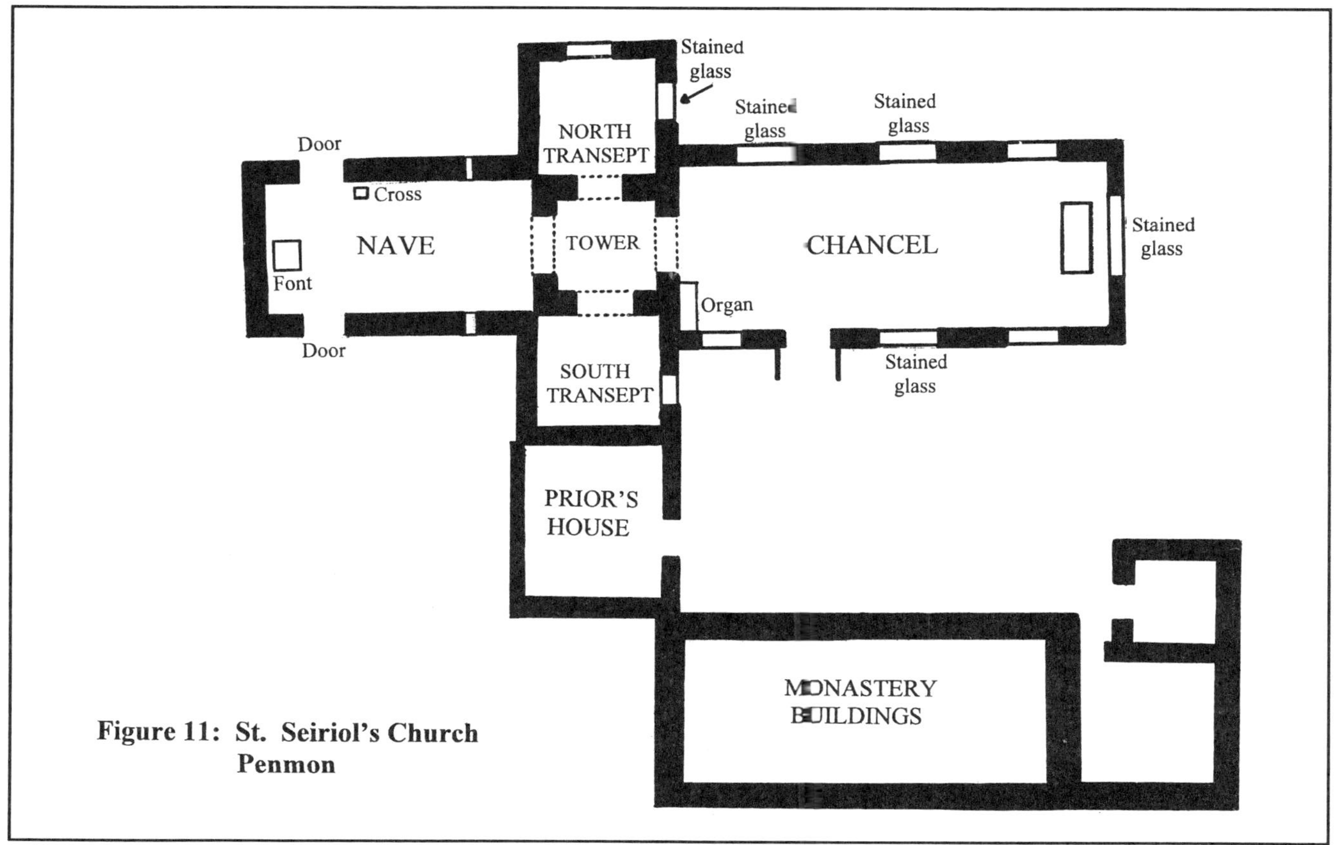

Figure 11: St. Seiriol's Church Penmon

a visit on account of its historic past, its architecture and its good state of repair. The monastic buildings surrounding the church date from 13th and 16th century and include the prior's house and the roofless ruins of refectory and dormitory. The foundations of St Seiriol's cell and his holy well are near the monastery's old fishpond located a few yards to the east of the church. [94]

Penmynydd – *St Credifael* (or ***Gredifael***)

The church is situated at the junction of two minor roads about 0.5 mile (0.8 km) north of the village of Penmynydd. Grid Reference SH 517 750.

The church was founded by St Credifael (or Gredifael, according to some) in the 6th century, and the first stone church was built here in the 12th century. The present church dates from the late 14th/early 15th century with the north chapel (the Tudor chapel) and the south porch dating from the 15th century. It was restored and refitted in 1848 under architect H. Longwith Jones. A further restoration was undertaken in 1969. Stones with chevron markings from an earlier church can be seen in the outside east and south walls of the chancel. The chancel has a south door; above it on the outside is a carved stone. The bell-cote has room for two bells although only one is in place. The steeply-pitched roof gives the interior of the church a sense of size and space; the interior walls are white-washed. The roof of the chancel is partly hidden by red panelling. In the north chapel is an alabaster table tomb dating from 1385 which is a memorial to Gronw Fychan ap Tudur ap Gronw and his wife Myfanwy of Plas Penmynydd. Gronw Fychan was an uncle of Owain Tudur who married Katherine de Valois (of the French royal family). Their son Edmund was the father of Henry VII who became the first Tudor king in 1485. It is believed that Gronw Fychan's tomb came from the Franciscan Friary at Llanfaes when it was dissolved in the 16th century. Ironically, it was Henry VIII, himself a Tudor king, who ordered the Dissolution of the Monasteries. The alabaster tomb has been extensively chipped because it was once believed that it had medicinal properties. The pew ends bear a fleur-de-lis design which reflect the connection between the Tudors and the French royal family. The plain octagonal font, near the west wall of the nave, is from the late 14th century. It has an eight-faced conical wooden cover. There is a silver tazza (saucer-shaped cup) which is dated 1573. It was given to the church by the family of Plas Penmynydd, along with a silver chalice in 1707. Also there is a pair of 19th century metal dog-tongs, about 1 metre long. The east window of the chancel dates from the early 15th century and contains stained glass. The middle light shows the crucifixion. The Tudor chapel has a small stained-glass window bearing a Tudor rose and the inscription 'Undeb fel rhosyn yw ar lan afonydd ac fel Tŷ Dur ar ben y mynydd' (Unity is like a rose on a river bank and like a house of steel on the mountain top). Tŷ Dur is a pun on the word Tudur (Tudor); similarly Pen y Mynydd (Mountain top) is simply the village name, Penmynydd. The Tudor chapel has a modern roof window. In the churchyard can be seen the grave of William Charles Owen (1881-1972), a well-known local figure better known as Llew Llwydiarth. On the south side of the church near the porch are some particularly old gravestones, one bearing the date 1618. [95]

Penrhoslligwy – ***St Michael/Sant Mihangel***

The church stands near a minor road 0.5 mile (0.8 km) west of the village of Brynrefail. It is necessary to walk across a small field before reaching the church. Grid Reference SH 481 859.

Penrhoslligwy was once the site of a royal court of the Princes of Gwynedd before the 1282 conquest by Edward I. It is possible, therefore, that the church may once have been a royal chapel. The east window, the north door and the chancel arch are believed to be from the 15th century; the chancel roof beams are medieval. The church was extensively restored by architects Henry Kennedy and John Rogers in 1865 when a north porch, a vestry and new windows were added. There are signs of very recent restoration work on the windows. The bell-cote houses one bell dated 1777. The only stained glass is in the 15th century east window of the chancel; the other windows are modern. The communion table dates from the 17th century. The font is an octagonal gritstone bowl of uncertain date. In the chancel can be seen an inscribed stone from the 6th century in memory of Maccudecceti. The inscription on the stone is *Hic iacit Maccudecceti* (Here lies Muccudecceti). Margaret Morris, the mother of the famous Morris brothers (William, Richard, Lewis and Siôn) of Pentre Eirianell, is commemorated by a tablet (1732) inside the church. Next to it was placed, in 2004, a tablet commemorating Siôn Morris (1713-1740), the youngest and least well-known of the brothers who died abroad. Some 45 victims of the 1859 Royal Charter disaster are buried in the churchyard (most of the others are buried at Llanallgo). The curate here at the time of the disaster was the Reverend Hugh Robert Hughes, a brother of the Reverend Stephen Roose Hughes (see Llanallgo). In the churchyard can also be seen an ancient cross believed to date from the 14th century. [96]

Penrhoslligwy – *Hen Gapel Lligwy*

The site is situated on a minor road 0.7 mile (1.1 km) north-east of the Llanallgo roundabout. Grid Reference SH 499 864.

Parts of this roofless chapel date back to the 12th century but with evidence of later additions. It may have been built as a memorial chapel and may have been connected to a Llys (Royal Court) at Penrhoslligwy. However, little is known for certain about its history or to which saint it was originally dedicated. The nave and chancel are undivided and the upper parts of the walls are mostly 14th century; the south doorway is probably 12th century. The south chapel and its crypt were added during the 16th century. Access to the crypt is by a flight of crudely-made steps. The bell-cote on the west wall is still in place. The internal walls still show clear signs of render. A large stone (about 2 feet square) with a socket at the top lies in the nave; this may have been the base of a cross at one time in the churchyard. Remains of the churchyard wall show that the chapel was within a roughly circular enclosure, typical of early churches. [97]

Pentraeth – *St Mary/Santes Fair*

This church is situated in the centre of the village at the junction of the A5025 and the B5109. Grid Reference SH 524 784.

Pentraeth was once known as Llanfair Betws Geraint. St Mary's church was extensively restored in 1821 and refitted in 1839. It was partly rebuilt under architect Henry Kennedy in 1882 when the porch was built and the chancel enlarged. Further restoration occurred in 1967. Parts of the nave and chancel walls are thought to be medieval. The north wall of the nave has a 17th century window. The east wall of the chancel contains a late 14th or early 15th century window. The south chapel dates from the 16th or 17th century and has a 17th century window in its east wall, the other windows being modern. The bell-cote contains one bell. Into the wall of the porch is fitted the bowl of an old font, believed to date from the 12th century. On the north side of the church is a blocked-up door. There are stained glass windows in the chancel and the south window of the chapel. The window in the chapel is dedicated to the memory of Claud Panton Vivian of Plas Gwyn who died in the Second World War, aged 24. The windows and the bell-cote are made of red sandstone and this shows signs of severe weathering in places. In the south side of the churchyard there is a large well-maintained plot containing graves of the Vivian family of nearby Plas Gwyn. This plot includes four beautifully-carved Celtic crosses. [98]

Puffin Island – (see Ynys Seiriol)

Rhodogeidio – ***St Ceidio***

This church is situated on a minor road 0.9 mile (1.5 km) north of Llannerch-y-medd. Grid Reference SH 412 855.

The name Rhodogeidio is thought to derive from 'rhodwydd Ceidio' – the defended mound of Ceidio. The church of St Ceidio stands on elevated ground in a pleasant, quiet rural location near the river Alaw. There are good views in all directions from this location; in the north east some 3 miles (5 km) distant can be seen the unmistakable features of the former copper mine of Mynydd Parys. The church, which is undivided into nave and chancel, stands within a small churchyard surrounded on the south side by trees. At one time it was a chapel of ease to Llantrisant church. The churchyard has a curved shape, typical of early Celtic churches. The site originally dates from the seventh century. The present building dates from 1845, but retains a 14th century east window. The 1845 rebuilding used materials from the previous church and was carried out under the direction of the Rector, the Reverend Hugh Wynne Jones. All the windows contain clear leaded glass. The bell-cote contains one bell, dated 1719. High in the west wall a curiously-shaped piece of slate has been inserted into the stonework. The church has no electricity supply and is lit by paraffin lamps. The font is a plain octagonal bowl on an octagonal base probably from the 15th century. The church has not been in regular use by the Church in Wales for some years, but it has been restored by the local community. Inside the church, the altar, lectern, pulpit, pews and font are still in place. The exterior remains in good condition with the door (in the north wall) having been replaced in 1995. [99]

Rhodogeidio – *St Mary/Santes Fair, Gwredog*

The church stands in an isolated location 1.5 miles (2.4 km) north-west of Llannerch-y-medd. Grid Reference SH 398 856.

Gwredog is an abbreviation of Llanfair yng Nghwaeredog (The church of St Mary on the sloping ground). The small church of St Mary was once a chapel of ease to Llantrisant church. This now redundant church stands 0.8 mile (1.3 km) west of Rhodogeidio church and has the distinction of probably being the most isolated church in Anglesey, being situated near the marshy land of Cors y Bol. It is undivided into nave and chancel and the total length is only about 30 feet (9 metres). The walls are from the 15th century but have been repaired and restored. The small east window is also from the 15th century. The bell was dated 1717. The church can only be reached on foot. It closed many years ago and is now a roofless ruin. [100]

Rhosbeirio – *St Peirio*

This church is situated on a minor road between Llanfechell and Rhosgoch. Grid Reference SH 391 917.

The small church of St Peirio is situated in a remote and quiet rural location. At one time it was a chapel of ease to Llaneilian church. A small gate leads to a grassy path lined on both sides by sycamore trees. The path widens into a circular churchyard containing a number of trees. The church is undivided into nave and chancel; parts of the walls may be medieval. Restoration of the church was financed by Richard Lloyd in 1812. Sadly the church closed a number of years ago and its windows are now boarded up, although the general fabric of the building including the roof appears to be in good condition. The bell-cote still contains its bell. Prior to its closure it housed a 12th century font in the form of a plain circular bowl. There is a fairly small number of gravestones (including a few from the 1980s and 1990s) in the churchyard which is in a surprisingly neat condition. [101]

Rhoscolyn – *St Gwenfaen*

The church stands in the village of Rhoscolyn in the south of Holy Island. Grid Reference SH 268 757.

This attractive little church stands in an elevated spot which overlooks a wide area of Anglesey as well as the mountains of the Llŷn peninsula. It is believed that St Gwenfaen's church was first established about 630 AD. A subsequent church built around the 15th century was destroyed by fire. At one time Rhoscolyn was an important church with chapels of ease at Llanfair yn Neubwll and Llanfihangel yn Nhowyn. Rhoscolyn has been called Llanwenfaen in the past. The present church is the result of reconstruction in 1871-75 using the masonry from the earlier 15th century church. The architect was the eminent Sir George Gilbert Scott who also restored Bangor Cathedral and St Cybi's Church, Holyhead. The 15th century doorway was inserted into the south wall of the new church and a porch added. The church was enlarged when the chancel was added in 1879, the architect being R.G. Thomas. The bell-cote contains a bell dated 1611. There is stained-glass in all the windows, including those in the porch. The font is a three-tier octagonal bowl from the 15th century. In the churchyard stands a monument to five crew members of the local lifeboat who died during a storm in December 1920 trying to rescue the crew of the 'Timbo'. Some distance from the church, on the west slope of Rhoscolyn head stands St Gwenfaen's Well (SH 259 754) having two sunken rooms including an enclosed pool. The well is credited with curing mental problems. Traditionally, an offering of two white quartz pebbles had to be made. [102]

Rhosneigr – *Christ Church/Eglwys Crist* (see Llanfaelog)

Rhosneigr – *Roman Catholic Church of our Lady & St Theresa/Eglwys Babyddol ein Harglwyddes a Santes Theresa*

The church is situated in Ffordd Maelog about 200 yards from the village clock. Grid Reference SH 319 730.

St Theresa's Church was established in 1957. It is a small neat-looking building with an asphalt roof and a stone frontage. There is a small flower garden in front and a car park to the rear. [103]

Rhosybol – *Christ Church/Eglwys Crist*

This church is situated at the roadside on the B5111 in the centre of the village. Grid Reference SH 426 883.

Rhosybol became a parish separate from Amlwch in 1873 and this church (designed by Henry Kennedy) was completed in 1875 to serve the growing community of Rhosybol. There was no previous church on the site. It is divided into nave and chancel. The porch is on the north side. The large ornate bell-cote contains one bell. There is stained glass in the nave and chancel. The church closed in about 1996 and the windows are now boarded. The churchyard, which contains a number of graves, is still well-maintained. [104]

Talwrn – *St Deiniol's Mission Church/ Eglwys Genhadol St Deiniol* (see Llanddyfnan)

Talyllyn – *St Mary/Santes Fair* (see Llanbeulan)

Trearddur Bay – *St Ffraid* (see Holyhead)

Trefdraeth – *St Beuno*

The church is situated on a minor road 0.9 mile (1.5 km) north of Malltraeth. Grid Reference SH 408 704.

The church is in a pleasant and quiet rural location. A simple lychgate leads to the churchyard. The church is fairly small with a roof of unusual ornately-shaped slates. The 14th century bell-cote houses one bell. The porch is on the south side. A slate tablet records that the present porch was built in 1761 and lists those who contributed financially to its construction. The chancel and nave (which are undivided) probably date from the 13th century. The east window of the chancel is late 14th or early 15th century; it contains stained glass. The south chapel is late 13th or early 14th century and has its own doorway on the west side. There is a stone archway between the south chapel and the rest of the church. There is also stained glass in the west and north walls. Inside the church are a number of memorials, one of them from the early 14th century. The font is a 12th century cylindrical bowl having six decorated panels. The wooden font cover is dated 1714. The church underwent repairs in 1846 and restoration in 1854 under Henry Kennedy. [105]

Trefdraeth – *Church of Christ the King/ Eglwys Crist y Brenin, Malltraeth*

This church is situated on a small site a short distance from the A4080 in the centre of Malltraeth. Grid Reference SH 406 688.

This tiny whitewashed church (in the parish of Trefdraeth) is not situated on a site of historical significance. It was built in 1874 to serve as an infants' school and a Mission Church. However, the school closed in 1913 and the building was subsequently used only as a mission church, known as St Elizabeth's Mission Church. In the late 1950s it underwent extensive restoration, with a new altar, furniture and floor. It was rededicated and became known as the Church of Christ the King in July 1959. The windows are of frosted glass with wooden frames. Above the porch is a bell-cote with one bell; the rope from the bell terminates in the porch. Inside the church, the nave and chancel are undivided. [106]

Tregaian – *St Caian*

The church is situated 2.5 miles (4.0 km) north of Llangefni, and 0.6 mile (1.0 km) off the B5111. Grid Reference SH 452 797.

This small church stands at the side of a minor road in a rural setting. The church and its churchyard are neat and well-maintained. The church is simply constructed with the continuous nave and chancel dating from the 14th century. The simple bell-cote contains one bell. The south door is 15th century. The windows in the north and south walls are square and contain clear leaded glass. In the east wall is a unusually wide single lancet window from the 14th century containing stained glass bearing the words 'Take unto you the whole armour of God'. Inside the church are wall tablets commemorating various members of the Lloyd family of nearby Plas Tregaian. The altar is a simple wooden table. The font is a 12th century circular tub-shaped bowl with chevron markings on the side. The wooden font cover bears an upright cross. On the south side of the churchyard near the church wall is the grave of William ap Howel who died in 1581, aged 105. He was married three times and had a total of 43 children, although some of these were not born in wedlock. At his funeral it is said that about three hundred members of the congregation were descended from him. [107]

Trewalchmai – *St Morhaiarn*

This church is situated a short distance south of the A5 in the village of Gwalchmai. Grid Reference SH 390 761.

The neat little church of St Morhaiarn is situated on elevated ground overlooking open countryside to the east. The nave and chancel of this church are continuous and underwent partial reconstruction in 1674, although much of it belongs to an earlier period. The north chapel was added in 1500; there are two arches between it and the rest of the church. The roofs are 17th century. The church underwent restoration in 1845 by the Rector, the Reverend J. Wynne Jones using some old materials. Old windows from St Llwydian's church, Heneglwys (which was undergoing restoration at the same time) were installed here in the east wall at that time. Further restoration, including rebuilding of the porch and installing some new windows, was completed by Henry Kennedy in 1885. The bell-cote contains one bell. The south doorway, believed to be from the 16th century, is blocked. All the windows have clear leaded panes, but there is a small amount of stained glass in the upper parts of the east window which is in three lights. This bears the inscription: Gwenwch yn ddibaid. Na ddiffoddwch yr ysbryd. (*Smile constantly. Do not extinguish the spirit*). The font is an octagonal bowl of unknown age. [108]

Valley – *St Michael/Sant Mihangel* (see Llanynghenedl)

Valley – *Our Lady's Roman Catholic Church/ Eglwys Babyddol Ein Harglwyddes, RAF Valley*

Grid Reference SH 315 765.

There has been a Catholic place of worship at RAF Valley since 1962. [109]

Ynys Seiriol

Ynys Seiriol (Puffin Island) is private property and there is no access.

Grid Reference SH 652 822.

The religious settlement originally founded by St Seiriol consisted of a 12th century church and some other monastic buildings. It was once occupied by a small community of monks of the Augustinian order. The only feature which remains, albeit in poor condition, is the central tower of the church. It has a squat pyramidal stone roof, rather like that of St Seiriol's Church, Penmon.